EYEWITNESS
ANIMAL

Totem pole featuring a thunderbird

Golden scarab beetle

Tree skink with regenerating tail

Seal skeleton

Tarantula

Blue-footed boobies

Ceramic statuette of Lipizzaner dancing horse

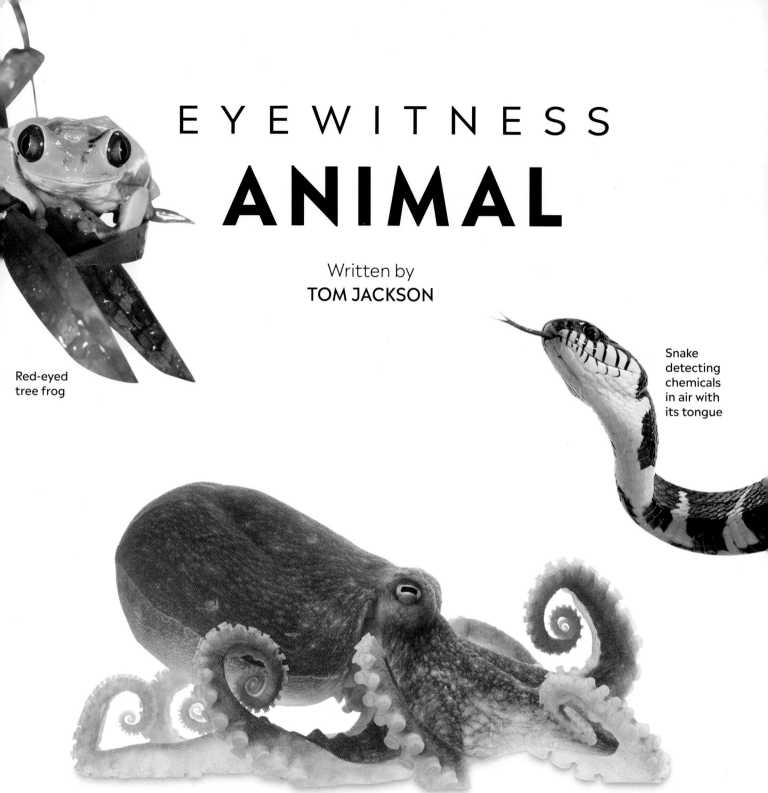

EYEWITNESS
ANIMAL

Written by
TOM JACKSON

Red-eyed
tree frog

Snake
detecting
chemicals
in air with
its tongue

Common octopus

Fisher's lovebirds

Penguin and chick

Penguin Random House

REVISED EDITION

DK DELHI
Senior Editor Rupa Rao **Senior Art Editor** Vikas Chauhan
Editor Zarak Rais **Art Editor** Astha Singh
Assistant Art Editors Abhimanyu Adhikary, Prateek Maurya
Team Lead, Picture Research Sumedha Chopra
Deputy Manager, Picture Research Virien Chopra
Managing Editor Kingshuk Ghoshal
Managing Art Editor Govind Mittal
DTP Designer Rakesh Kumar **Production Editor** Pawan Kumar
Jacket Designers Juhi Sheth, Rhea Menon
Senior Jackets Coordinator Priyanka Sharma Saddi
DK India Creative Head Malavika Talukder

DK LONDON
Senior Editor Rona Skene
Art Editor Beth Johnston
Senior US Editor Megan Douglass
US Executive Editor Lori Cates Hand
Managing Editor Francesca Baines
Managing Art Editor Philip Letsu
Production Controller Jack Matts
Jacket Design Development Manager Sophia MTT
Publisher Andrew Macintyre
Art Director Mabel Chan
Managing Director Sarah Larter

Consultant Dr. Michael Leach

FIRST EDITION

DK DELHI
Project Editor Bharti Bedi **Project Art Editor** Deep Shikha Walia
Senior Editor Kingshuk Ghoshal **Senior Art Editor** Govind Mittal
Senior DTP Designer Tarun Sharma
DTP Designer Neeraj Bhatia **DTP Manager** Sunil Sharma
Deputy Managing Editor Eman Chowdhary
Managing Art Editor Romi Chakraborty
Production Manager Pankaj Sharma
Jacket Designer Govind Mittal

DK LONDON
Senior Editor Dr. Rob Houston **Senior Art Editor** Philip Letsu
Publisher Andrew Macintyre
Picture Researcher Myriam Mégharbi
Production Editor Ben Marcus
Production Controller Luca Frassinetti
US Editor Margaret Parrish

This American Edition, 2024
First American Edition, 2012
Published in the United States by DK Publishing,
a division of Penguin Random House LLC
1745 Broadway, 20th Floor, New York, NY 10019

A catalog record for this book is available from the
Library of Congress.
ISBN 978-0-5938-4381-9 (Paperback)
ISBN 978-0-5938-4382-6 (ALB)

DK books are available at special discounts when purchased in bulk
for sales promotions, premiums, fund-raising, or educational use.
For details, contact: DK Publishing Special Markets,
1745 Broadway, 20th Floor, New York, NY 10019
SpecialSales@dk.com

Printed and bound in China

www.dk.com

European common frog

Blue morpho butterfly

Cuvier's Toucan

Homo habilis, a human ancestor

Contents

Serval cat

What is an animal?

Only about 1.3 million of Earth's animal species have been identified. They range from tigers to dust mites, and even sea anemones and sponges. Each animal is made up of millions, if not billions, of cells. What sets animals apart from other many-celled organisms is that they are more mobile and survive by eating other life forms.

A species

Every animal belongs to a species. Its members look similar, and share the same lifestyle and habitats. They can breed with each other and produce young. The color, size, and body shape of this emerald tree boa help other snakes and scientists identify it.

Development plan

Every animal grows from a single cell that divides repeatedly. Most animals, such as this terrapin, develop bilaterally, with a mouth at one end and a rear opening at the other. Some simple animals, such as anemones, develop outward from a central point.

Green sea anemone

Line that divides animal into equal halves

Line of symmetry divides animal into equal halves.

Red-eared terrapin

Animal cell

All living bodies are formed of tiny units called cells. An animal cell contains structures called organelles, which form its factories, power supply, and chemical transportation system. It is surrounded by a flexible membrane.

Mitochondrion produces a cell's energy.

Liquid cytoplasm fills cell.

Nucleus houses cell's genes.

The animal kingdom

The system of organizing life into groups was developed by Swedish biologist Carl Linnaeus. He split the animal kingdom into subgroups based on their shared features. Phylum is the largest subgroup, followed by class, order, family, genus, and then species. Every animal has a unique scientific name, formed by its genus and species.

Classification of some salamander species

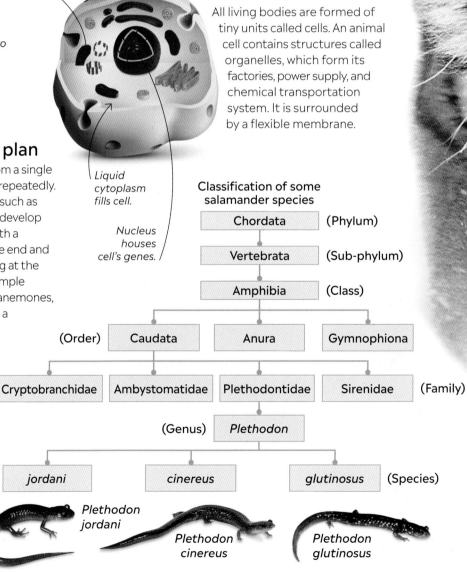

Chordata		(Phylum)
Vertebrata		(Sub-phylum)
Amphibia		(Class)

(Order)	Caudata	Anura	Gymnophiona

Cryptobranchidae	Ambystomatidae	Plethodontidae	Sirenidae	(Family)

(Genus)	*Plethodon*

jordani	*cinereus*	*glutinosus*	(Species)

Plethodon jordani

Plethodon cinereus

Plethodon glutinosus

Ear and other sense organs give the tiger information about its surroundings.

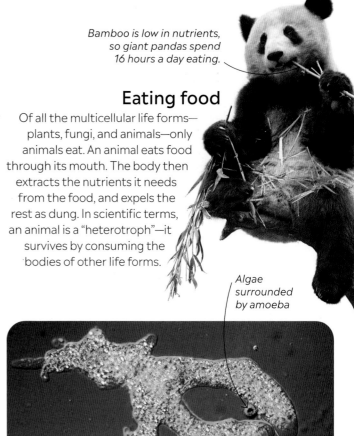

Bamboo is low in nutrients, so giant pandas spend 16 hours a day eating.

Eating food

Of all the multicellular life forms—plants, fungi, and animals—only animals eat. An animal eats food through its mouth. The body then extracts the nutrients it needs from the food, and expels the rest as dung. In scientific terms, an animal is a "heterotroph"—it survives by consuming the bodies of other life forms.

Algae surrounded by amoeba

Almost an animal

Perhaps the closest life forms to animals are some microscopic, single-celled organisms, including amoebas. These organisms can surround and engulf tinier prey.

Going mobile

Animals are the only many-celled organisms that can move from place to place. Most plants are rooted to something. Locomotion is usually a response to changes in the environment. It is possible because an animal does not have rigid body cells.

WEBS OF FOOD

Living things in any environment are interconnected in food webs that link everything edible. It begins with producers, such as plants and bacteria—organisms that make their own food using energy from sunlight. Energy is then transferred to the primary consumers that feed on the producers, and so on.

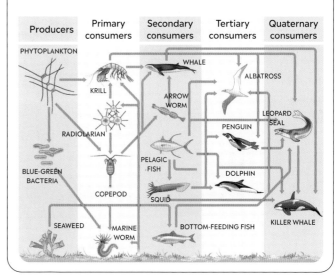

Invertebrates

An invertebrate is an animal without vertebrae, or spine bones. These were the first animals on Earth, appearing in the oceans at least 700 million years ago. More than 95 percent of animals alive today are invertebrates, which include more than 20 groups.

Simple sponges

Sponges may be similar to the first invertebrates on Earth. Their simple bodies are made up of just a few cell types. Pore cells let water in, cone cells sift the food from it, and other cell types build the skeleton.

Blooming animals

Sea anemones are often mistaken for plants and are even named after a type of flower, but they are carnivorous animals. Anemones, jellyfish, and several other invertebrates have circular bodies, and no head.

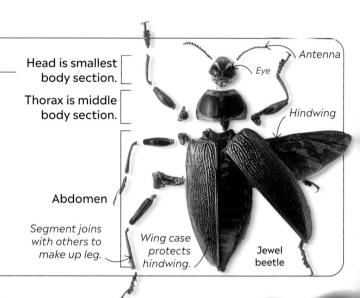

IN SECTIONS

The body of an arthropod is divided into segments. In insects—the world's biggest animal group with more than 1 million species—some segments have fused (joined) together during evolution to form body sections. Insect bodies have three main sections—the head, thorax, and abdomen.

Head is smallest body section.

Thorax is middle body section.

Abdomen

Segment joins with others to make up leg.

Antenna

Eye

Hindwing

Wing case protects hindwing.

Jewel beetle

Stinging tentacles look like petals.

Many mollusks

The second-largest invertebrate group are the mollusks, with 100,000 species. All mollusk bodies have one muscular "foot" to move, and the organs are held inside a mantle (a fleshy hood). Most mollusks have a hard shell made with a mineral called calcium carbonate, but several types, such as sea slugs, live without a shell.

Mantle changes color to blend in with surroundings.

Octopuses have eight tentacles lined with suckers.

Cephalopods

The largest invertebrates are the cephalopods— a group of mollusks without shells that includes octopuses, squid, and cuttlefish. Most of the body is the bulging mantle, while the foot is divided into flexible tentacles covered in suckers.

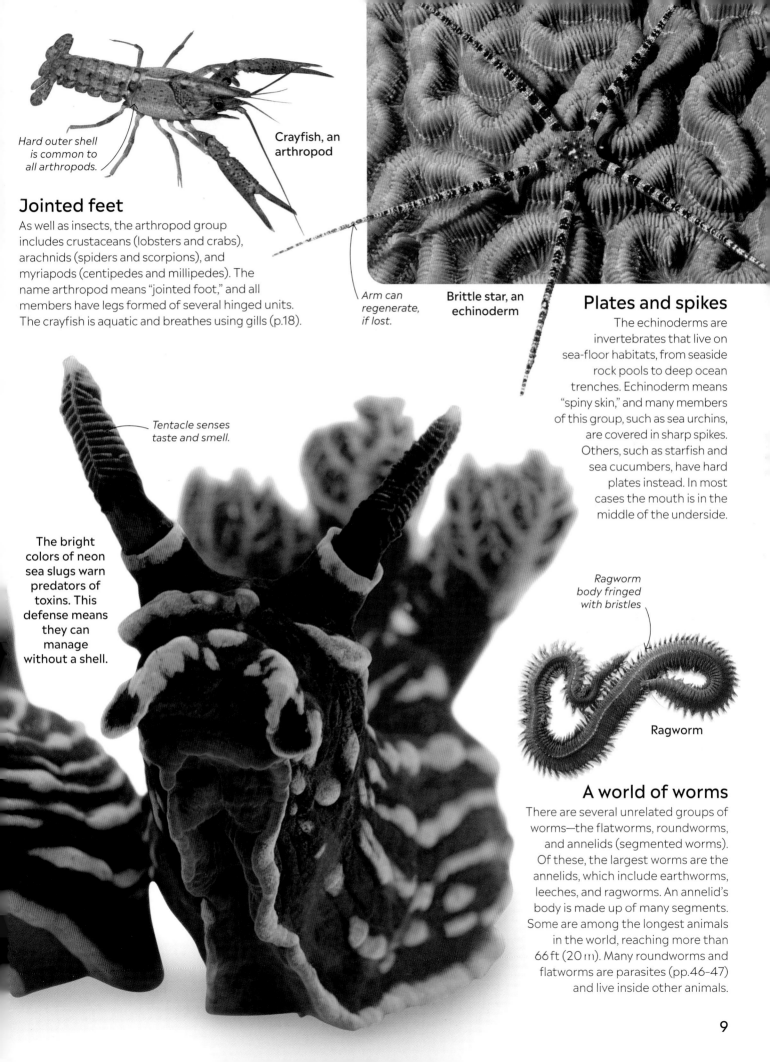

Crayfish, an arthropod

Hard outer shell is common to all arthropods.

Jointed feet

As well as insects, the arthropod group includes crustaceans (lobsters and crabs), arachnids (spiders and scorpions), and myriapods (centipedes and millipedes). The name arthropod means "jointed foot," and all members have legs formed of several hinged units. The crayfish is aquatic and breathes using gills (p.18).

Arm can regenerate, if lost.

Brittle star, an echinoderm

Plates and spikes

The echinoderms are invertebrates that live on sea-floor habitats, from seaside rock pools to deep ocean trenches. Echinoderm means "spiny skin," and many members of this group, such as sea urchins, are covered in sharp spikes. Others, such as starfish and sea cucumbers, have hard plates instead. In most cases the mouth is in the middle of the underside.

Tentacle senses taste and smell.

The bright colors of neon sea slugs warn predators of toxins. This defense means they can manage without a shell.

Ragworm body fringed with bristles

Ragworm

A world of worms

There are several unrelated groups of worms—the flatworms, roundworms, and annelids (segmented worms). Of these, the largest worms are the annelids, which include earthworms, leeches, and ragworms. An annelid's body is made up of many segments. Some are among the longest animals in the world, reaching more than 66 ft (20 m). Many roundworms and flatworms are parasites (pp.46-47) and live inside other animals.

Cold-blooded vertebrates

The vertebrates are animals with a chain of bony segments running down the middle of their backs, forming a backbone. Each spine bone is called a vertebra. Fish, amphibians, and reptiles are all ectothermic, or "cold-blooded," vertebrates. Ectotherms cannot maintain a constant body temperature and rely on their surroundings to keep them warm.

Throat pouch puffed out to make calls

Spring king
Amphibians were the first land vertebrates. They are the ancestors of all tetrapods—animals with four limbs—including those with wings. Although early tetrapods also had short, rigid necks, they looked nothing like modern frogs. With their very long back legs, frogs are built to jump.

Cartilage is **lighter** than bone, allowing **sharks** to **swim fast** without using too much energy.

Without bone
A vertebrate's body gets its shape from its internal skeleton. In most cases, the skeleton is made of hard bone. However, sharks have bones built of cartilage, which is made from flexible protein.

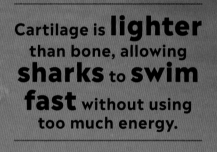

Rays of bone
Most fish have ray fins formed from skin stretched over slim shafts of bone. Ray fins are ideal for wafting water, but are too weak to hold a fish's weight. Land vertebrates evolved from another group called lobe-finned fish, which have fleshy fins and thick bones.

Life without legs
Not having legs makes it easier for snakes to slide through narrow burrows and slither over loose sand. Strong species, such as this cobra, can even rise up to stare into the eyes of taller animals.

Large thigh muscle powers jump.

Moist skin lets oxygen and water through.

High and dry

Reptiles were the first vertebrates to adopt a life away from water. They have waterproof scales and their eggs have a tough, protective shell. They are cold-blooded and cannot heat their own bodies, so many reptiles, such as this Agama lizard, must regularly bask in the sun to survive.

Webbed feet to aid swimming

A dorsal fin helps a shark balance when it attacks its prey.

Long leg bones lever frog forward.

 EYEWITNESS

Keertana Jillella
After an encounter with a snake in her community, US school student Keertana developed an app called "HawkEYE." It controls a machine that scans spaces for snakes, then photographs and identifies them. Venomous snakes are then driven back with a jet of water.

Between two worlds

Most amphibians live two lives. They start out in water, hatching from eggs laid in pools. Young amphibians (larvae), such as this spotted salamander (above), breathe through gills and swim with fins, like fish. As they mature, they grow legs for walking on land and most develop lungs for breathing air.

Warm-blooded
vertebrates

Birds and mammals are the only endothermic, or "warm-blooded," animals. Endothermic means "heat within." Endotherms can regulate their body temperature and keep warmer than their surroundings using fur, fat, or feathers to trap heat. Because of temperature controls, such as sweating, their body works well in most environments.

Flightless

The kiwi lives in New Zealand. Until humans arrived 750 years ago, it had no mammal predators, such as cats. The kiwi had no need to fly and did not develop a breastbone that could support strong flight muscles—making it a type of flightless bird called a ratite.

Quill has tiny barbs that make it painful to pull out when stuck in skin.

Spikes and tufts

Mammal hair is sometimes put to unusual uses. For example, the defensive spikes, or quills, of a porcupine are very thick hairs. When threatened, a porcupine raises its quills, making itself appear larger than it is. Most of the quills point backward, so if a predator attacks from behind, it gets a sharp shock.

Flight feather extends back from bone at front of wing.

Porcupine quills

Flexible feathers

A bird's plumage, or covering of feathers, has several functions. Fluffy down feathers close to the skin trap air, creating a blanket of warm air around the body. The long, stiff, and very light feathers are used for flight. Feathers may be drab to provide camouflage, or highly colorful, as in this macaw, to attract mates.

Electron micrograph of fox fur (false color)

Electron micrograph of feather (false color)

Feather vs hair

Hair and feathers are made of a protein called keratin. Mammal hairs have different lengths. The short underfur insulates, while longer guard hairs keep water and dirt out. Feathers are more complex. The strands branch out from a central shaft, before dividing again to form thin fibers that hook together to make a flat surface.

Lumbar vertebra
(backbone)

Cranium
(skull)

Cervical
vertebra
(neck bone)

Mandible
(jawbone)

Rib

Caudal
vertebra
(tail
bone)

**Skeleton of
gray wolf**

Ulna

Radius

Phalanx
(toe bone)

Cranium
(skull)

Cervical
vertebra
(neck bone)

Lumbar
vertebra
(backbone)

Mandible
(jawbone)

Caudal
vertebra
(tail bone)

Rib

Ulna

Radius

**Skeleton of
harbor seal**

Phalanx
(toe bone)

One skeleton fits all

The mammals are a diverse group. Wolves are built for a life on the run, while seals are at home in the water. However, all mammals have the same set of bones. The seal's flippers are merely longer, flatter versions of the wolf's springlike feet.

Laying eggs

Most mammals give birth to live young. Placentals nurture young inside their bodies (with a placenta), while marsupials give birth to immature young and nurture them inside a pouch. Only five mammal species, including this duck-billed platypus, lay eggs. They form the group called monotremes.

Long, colored
tail feather

Forward-facing
eye

Primates

This mandrill is a primate. The primates are placental mammals, and include monkeys, lemurs, apes, and humans. They evolved in the treetops, and their big brains, long limbs, and grasping hands were useful for life in the branches. Forward-facing eyes provide binocular vision for judging distances.

Orca breaches
surface of water.

Mammals in water

Several mammal groups have evolved to survive in the water. Some, such as sea lions, still spend time on land, but the cetaceans (whales and dolphins) never set foot on shore. They have flippers in place of forelegs and no hind limbs at all. Cetaceans include the orcas, or killer whales.

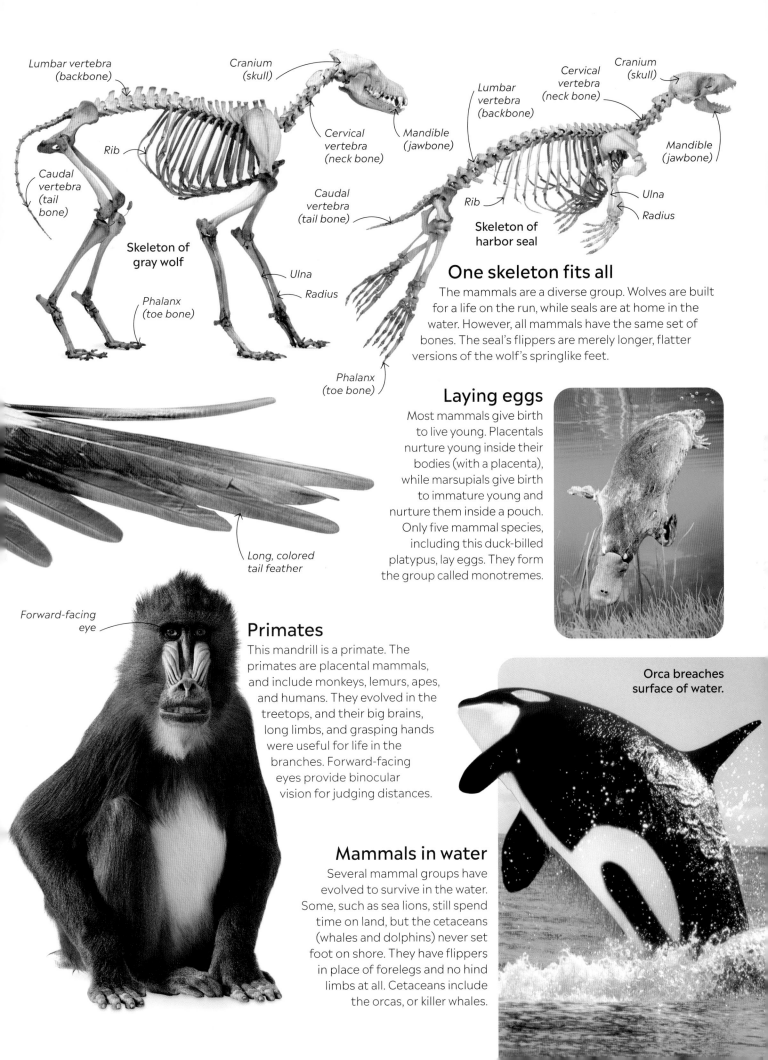

Evolution

Every species seems to be a perfect fit for its way of life. A sea snake has a flat, paddle-shaped tail that helps it swim, while a burrowing snake has a shovel-shaped snout suited to digging through soil. But both snakes have changed over time, evolving adaptations that better shape them to their environments. The driving force of this process is called natural selection.

Inherited features

The instructions for making a body are coded in genes—a set of chemicals called deoxyribonucleic acid (DNA) held in every cell. Parents pass genes (and their traits) to their offspring, giving the young an advantage (or disadvantage) over others. Those with desirable genes do well and have many young. Their DNA becomes more common.

Thymine (T)

Adenine (A)

Cytosine (C)

Guanine (G)

The backbone of DNA is made of sugar molecules.

Genes are strands of DNA coded with the chemical units, or bases, A, C, T, and G.

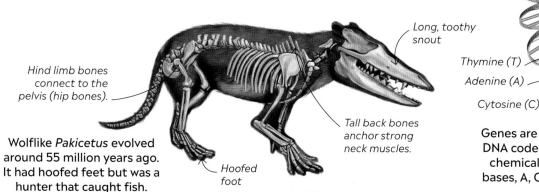

Hind limb bones connect to the pelvis (hip bones).

Long, toothy snout

Tall back bones anchor strong neck muscles.

Hoofed foot

Wolflike *Pakicetus* evolved around 55 million years ago. It had hoofed feet but was a hunter that caught fish.

Powerful tail helps to swim.

Legs used to swim and walk on land

Webbed foot

Jawbone picks up sounds like a modern whale.

Crocodile-like *Ambulocetus* lived 50 million years ago.

Extended body

Blind progress

Evolution is continuous, and doesn't only travel in one direction. For example, mammals evolved from animals whose ancestors were fish. Much later, some mammals began pursuing a watery lifestyle. Their legs slowly evolved into flippers and their bodies became fish-shaped. The result was whales.

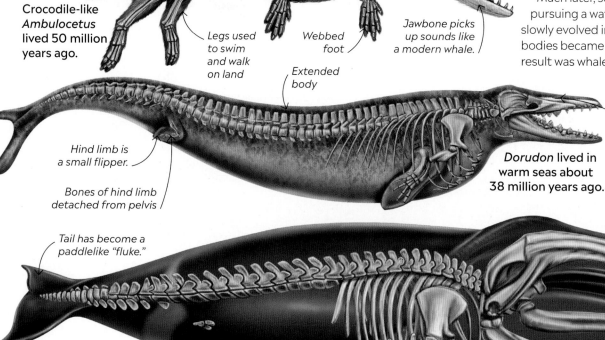

Hind limb is a small flipper.

Bones of hind limb detached from pelvis

Nostril halfway along snout

Dorudon lived in warm seas about 38 million years ago.

Large skull helps break Arctic ice.

Tail has become a paddlelike "fluke."

Balaena—the modern bowhead whale—has the largest mouth of any animal.

Tiny hind limb bones

Flipper

Charles Darwin

In 1859, English scientist Charles Darwin (1809–1882) put forward the idea of evolution by natural selection in his book *On the Origin of Species*. He discovered that finches on different Galápagos Islands had evolved different-shaped beaks to suit the food available on each island. These observations led to his revolutionary theory.

Coevolution

Some organisms evolve together in a process called coevolution. Acacia ants have coevolved with the bullhorn acacia shrub. The ants protect the plant from being eaten, and in return, the plant provides the ants with nectar and an edible nodule.

Small, spiky thorn

Ants on patrol

Never the same

Natural selection exists because no two animals are the same. Even members of the same species—such as these ladybugs—are at least slightly different because they have a unique set of genes. Despite their warning patterns, a bird may eat one of the bugs. The other may survive and produce offspring.

Azara's agouti collects fruits and roots on rainforest floor.

The gray squirrel harvests nuts from trees.

The Arabian spiny mouse forages for seeds in grasses.

Radiating species

These rodents evolved from a single ancestor that lived 65 million years ago, but the descendants have evolved in different directions. This "adaptive radiation" gives rise to a whole range of new species that live in diverse habitats but share features, such as gnawing front teeth.

This wildebeest has reacted slower than its herd mates.

Survival of the fittest

Darwin described animals that were able to survive and reproduce as being "fit." In these terms, a fit animal is not just strong and healthy, its behavior also makes it successful at surviving and reproducing in ways that perfectly fit the habitat. These cheetahs are "fit" because they have got within pouncing distance of a wildebeest.

Extinct animals

About 99 percent of all species that have ever lived on Earth are extinct. Over the last 700 million years, the animal kingdom has constantly changed, with new species taking the place of older ones. Animals may become extinct naturally when there is a disaster, when members of a species fail to reproduce, or when a new species evolves and is more successful in the struggle for survival.

Echmatocrinus, a primitive echinoderm

This extinct sea reptile's large eyes show that it dived into dark waters.

An explosion of life

A great blooming of species—called the Cambrian Explosion—happened around 530 million years ago (MYA). Almost all animals living today—from fish to fleas—had an ancestor that once swam in the ocean during this period. All of the Cambrian species, including the invertebrates seen below, are now extinct, but they paved the way for the animal diversity we see today.

Studying fossils

Everything we know about extinct animals comes from fossils, which are the remains of animals, their footprints, and droppings, preserved in rocks. It is rare for whole skeletons to be preserved—paleontologists (fossil scientists) build up a picture of how the animal looked and lived from fragments of bone.

Opabinia (possibly a giant ancestor of a tardigrade)

Haikouichthys, one of the earliest vertebrates

Marrella (thought to be a primitive arthropod)

Corythosaurus,
a dinosaur

Mass extinctions

Extinctions may occur due to a global catastrophe that kills thousands of species at once. Earth has witnessed at least five mass extinctions, the last of which occurred 66 million years ago (MYA) when the dinosaurs died out. The worst extinction of all was the one around 250 MYA, which wiped out most life.

👁 **EYEWITNESS**

Dr. Darren Naish
British zoologist Darren Naish specializes in the study of dinosaurs and pterosaurs (flying reptiles) in Earth's Cretaceous Period. He has provided scientific advice on several TV shows. He has a fossilized fish, *Scalacurvichthys naishi*, named after him.

Homo habilis made cutting tools out of flakes of stone.

Extinct humans

Our species, *Homo sapiens*, is not the first human species, but it is the only one that has not died out. One earlier species was *Homo habilis*, or "handy man," which lived between 2.4 and 1.4 MYA.

Dead end

Some extinctions spell the end for an entire group of animals. The one 250 MYA wiped out the trilobites, which were once common in the sea.

Armor plates on a trilobite's back allowed it to roll up for protection.

Killed by humans

The thylacine, or marsupial tiger, became extinct in 1936 when the last one died in an Australian zoo. By then, all wild thylacines—predators more closely related to kangaroos than cats—had been shot, because they were considered pests.

Anomalocaris, a primitive arthropod

Wiwaxia, a primitive annelid

Hallucigenia (possibly a velvet worm)

Body systems

Like a machine, an animal's body must be supplied with fuel and raw materials. It must also get rid of waste and repair itself when damaged. To carry out these functions, most animals have a basic set of body systems, each managing one set of life processes—digesting food, transporting nutrients and waste, moving, and protecting the body. Different animal bodies perform the same jobs in different ways.

Body framework

For land animals, a rigid skeleton allows them to raise their body parts against the pull of gravity. It also provides anchor points for muscles to pull on, allowing animals to move their bodies. A vertebrate has an internal skeleton, but an insect, such as this beetle, has a hard exoskeleton (skeleton outside the body).

Crab spider drinks fleshy soup.

The flow of blood

Without a supply of blood and the oxygen it contains, an animal's body parts would soon start to die. As well as cells carrying oxygen, blood carries a range of chemicals. These include hormones—chemical messengers that control body systems. For many animals, like this glass frog, blood travels inside special vessels that form the main chemical transportation network.

Heart pumps blood around body.

Pouch is full of water so gills work even above water level.

Meat soup

Usually after swallowing food, an animal must digest it to break it down into sugars, fats, and proteins. It uses these substances as fuel or to build up the body. Digestion is mostly done by powerful chemicals in the stomach and intestines called enzymes. A spider, however, pumps its stomach enzymes into prey, turning the victim's insides into a fleshy soup, which it then sucks up.

Gas exchange

Animals take in oxygen and give out carbon dioxide in a process called gas exchange. Oxygen chemically breaks down sugar, releasing energy, and producing carbon dioxide as waste. Simple animals exchange gases through the surface of their bodies, but larger ones have lungs or, like this mudskipper, gills.

**Body organs
seen through
the belly of a
glass frog**

Brain chain

The body's main communication
system is made up of nerves, which work
like wires carrying electric signals. The nerves
connect to ganglion "junction boxes," which
take care of different body sections. Vertebrates
have a centralized nervous system under the control
of a brain, while insects, such as this
cockroach, have a chain of nearly
independent ganglia.

*Nerve connects
to muscle.*

*Single
ganglion
controls
body part.*

*Body shortens
when longitudinal
muscles contract.*

**Leech
pulled
into a ball**

*Circular muscles
contract to
lengthen body.*

**Leech
extends
its head.**

*Body flattens
as longitudinal
muscles relax.*

Sucker anchors body.

**Body
is fully
stretched.**

Pull and stretch

Animals move using muscles, which are built up from
tiny fibers of protein. When muscles receive an electric
pulse from a nerve, they shorten, for example drawing
this leech into a ball. Muscles cannot push, so they work
in pairs, in which one set produces the opposite
movement to the other.

*Vein returns
blood to heart.*

*See-through
skin on belly*

**Blue skin warns this
frog is poisonous.**

**Stripes hide a tiger
in dry grasses.**

Clever skin

Skin is a tough but highly sensitive
barrier, alerting an animal to cold,
heat, and the slightest touch. It is also a
self-repairing structure that acts as the
first line of defense against diseases.
Skin takes many forms, ranging from
waterproof reptile scales and breathable
amphibian skin, to the hair- and feather-
covered skin of birds and mammals.

**Crocodile scales
have bony plates.**

**Bright parrot plumage
attracts mates.**

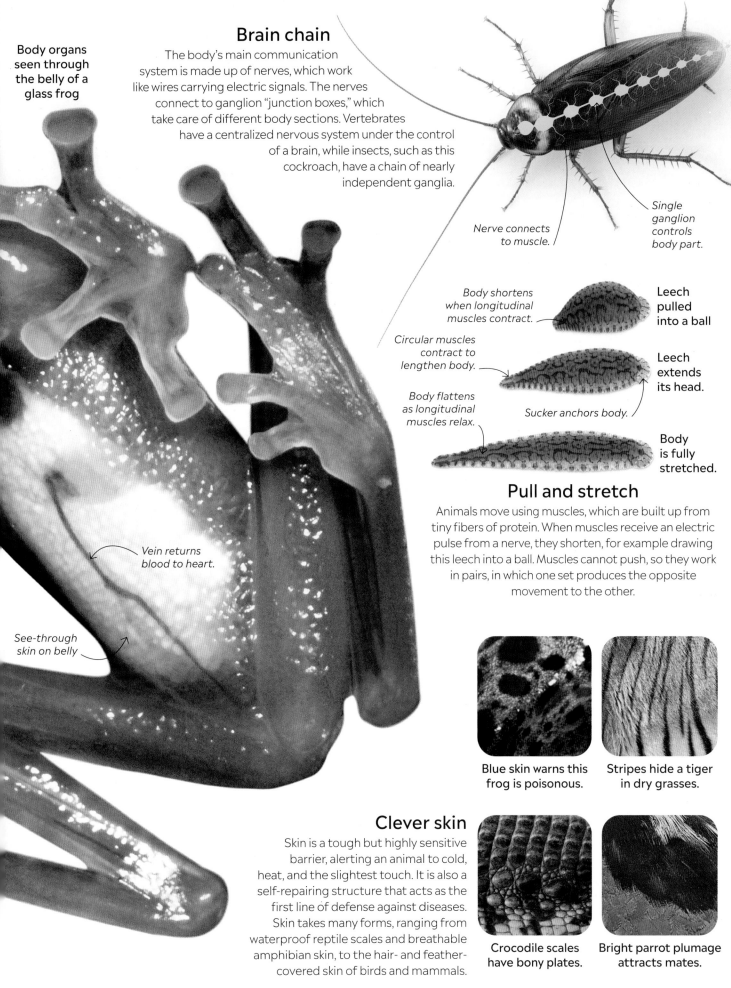

19

Senses

In order to survive, an animal needs to gather information about its surroundings. It must search for its meals, watch for threatening predators, and find a member of its own species to mate with. An animal builds up information from its senses to make split-second decisions that could make the difference between life and death.

All eyes

Tarsiers are primates, with a body no bigger than a person's hand. Its eyes take up more room in its head than its brain, but it needs these huge eyes to collect enough light to hunt insects at night.

Each eye has 10,000 lenses.

Vibrissae (whiskers)

Eyes can see heat and ultraviolet light, both invisible to humans.

Space detectors

A mouse can search for food in total darkness thanks to its vibrissae—touch-sensitive hairs that stick out from its snout. It uses these whiskers to judge the width of gaps, knowing if they fit, its body will too.

Multicolored world

Eyes detect light using chemicals called pigments. Each pigment triggers an electric pulse when hit by a blip of light energy. The pulse travels along nerves to the brain, which builds a picture from many pulses. The most complex eyes belong to the mantis shrimp. Its eye has 12 pigments, compared to only three in the human eye.

Dish face

A nocturnal owl hunts silently at night. Its wings make no noise as it swoops in for a kill. The owl targets its prey carefully: it collects faint sounds using the disk of feathers around the face, which works like a satellite dish. The facial disk focuses the sound into the owl's ears beneath the feathers.

SCANNER SYSTEM

Sharks are sensitive to electric signals produced by their prey. Muscle movements generate weak electric fields that surround the shark's victims in the water. These signals are picked up by tiny pits, called ampullae of Lorenzini, dotted around the shark's snout. The ampullae even allow sharks to scan for prey buried in sand.

Jelly in ampullae converts electric signals into nerve pulses.

Prey

Nerve carries pulses to brain.

Faint electric field produced by prey's muscles

Feathery antenna traps chemicals floating in the air.

Pointed tip of tongue collects scent chemicals in the air.

Fire beetle and its sensors

Hot spotters

Most animals run away from forest fires, but a fire beetle heads straight for them. Its tiny heat sensors can pinpoint a major fire from 7½ miles (12 km) away. This beetle lays its eggs in freshly burned trees.

Tasting air

Most snakes rely on their smell senses to find food. As well as sniffing the air, a snake tastes it by flicking out its long, forked tongue. It then slots the tips into a scent detector—Jacobson's organ—on the roof of its mouth. This organ detects which tip has more scent on it, and in which direction prey lies.

Scent feelers

Antennae—the "feelers" on an invertebrate's head—are mostly used to feel objects. However, male moths use their feathery antennae to sweep the air for smells, especially the special scent chemicals released by females.

Animal diets

Diet is a deciding factor in what an animal looks like and how it survives. Some species exploit one food source, while others survive on whatever comes their way. For instance, the snail kite is a small, predatory bird that swoops over marshlands preying only on snails. In contrast, the Andean condor is an immense bird that glides for miles in search of a meal. It will eat anything, from the carcass of a beached whale to a nest full of eggs.

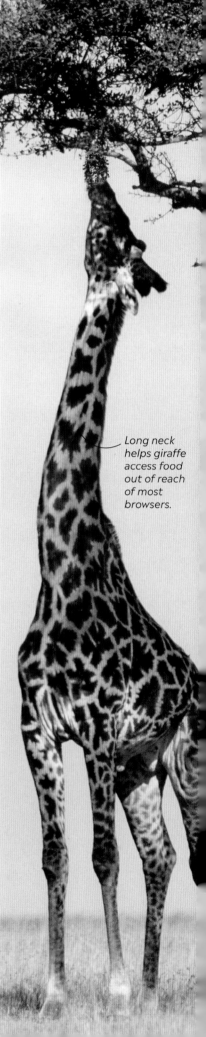

Long neck helps giraffe access food out of reach of most browsers.

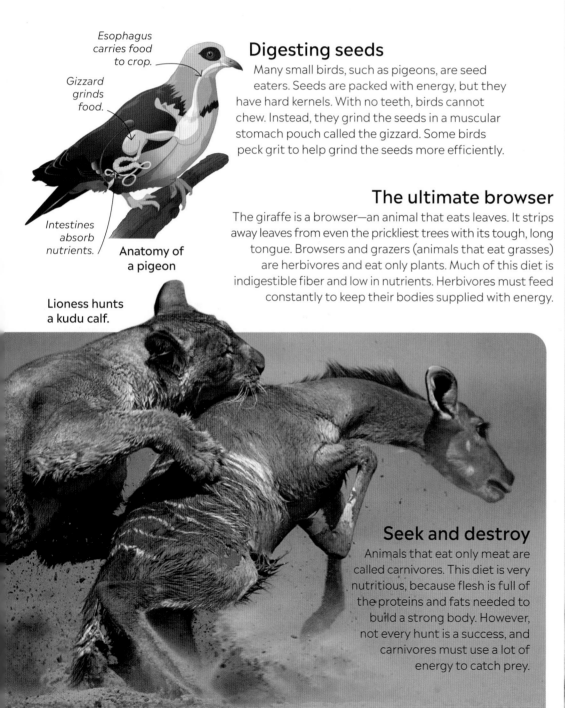

Esophagus carries food to crop.

Gizzard grinds food.

Intestines absorb nutrients.

Anatomy of a pigeon

Digesting seeds

Many small birds, such as pigeons, are seed eaters. Seeds are packed with energy, but they have hard kernels. With no teeth, birds cannot chew. Instead, they grind the seeds in a muscular stomach pouch called the gizzard. Some birds peck grit to help grind the seeds more efficiently.

The ultimate browser

The giraffe is a browser—an animal that eats leaves. It strips away leaves from even the prickliest trees with its tough, long tongue. Browsers and grazers (animals that eat grasses) are herbivores and eat only plants. Much of this diet is indigestible fiber and low in nutrients. Herbivores must feed constantly to keep their bodies supplied with energy.

Lioness hunts a kudu calf.

Seek and destroy

Animals that eat only meat are called carnivores. This diet is very nutritious, because flesh is full of the proteins and fats needed to build a strong body. However, not every hunt is a success, and carnivores must use a lot of energy to catch prey.

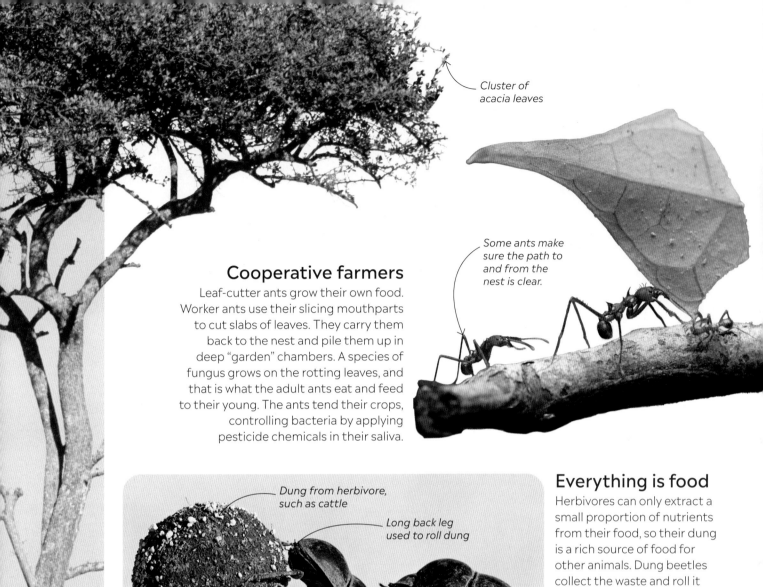

*Cluster of
acacia leaves*

Cooperative farmers

Leaf-cutter ants grow their own food.
Worker ants use their slicing mouthparts
to cut slabs of leaves. They carry them
back to the nest and pile them up in
deep "garden" chambers. A species of
fungus grows on the rotting leaves, and
that is what the adult ants eat and feed
to their young. The ants tend their crops,
controlling bacteria by applying
pesticide chemicals in their saliva.

*Some ants make
sure the path to
and from the
nest is clear.*

*Dung from herbivore,
such as cattle*

*Long back leg
used to roll dung*

Everything is food

Herbivores can only extract a
small proportion of nutrients
from their food, so their dung
is a rich source of food for
other animals. Dung beetles
collect the waste and roll it
into balls, inside which they
lay their eggs. When the
grubs hatch, they have
a ready food supply.

Flesh of the dead

Animals that eat carrion—the flesh of dead
animals—are called scavengers. A vulture
is a top scavenger. It patrols the skies on
wide wings, and its hooked beak is ideal for
ripping scraps of flesh from bones.

**Rüppell's
vulture**

Curiosity pays

Opportunist feeders never miss a chance to
eat a meal. They are usually omnivores—
animals that eat plants and animals, dead or
alive. The curious coati checks every nook and
cranny with its long nose and sensitive forepaws.

Female   Male

Parenting

An animal that dies without reproducing cannot pass on its genes. In nature, the only species that survive are those that are driven to reproduce. Most animals use sexual reproduction, in which a male and female pair up to mix both of their traits. This creates variation and increases the chances that some offspring will survive. After hatching or being born, the young begin to grow.

Courting a mate

Strong, healthy animals make the best mates because it is likely that their offspring will be healthy too. The male blue-footed booby puts on a show for a potential mate by spreading his wings and stamping his feet. The deep blue color of the feet is a sign that this male is healthy.

Precious cargo

An animal needs to ensure that its offspring survive long enough to reproduce themselves. Unlike most invertebrates, scorpions produce only a few eggs. The offspring spend the first part of their lives on their mother's back. She protects her newborns so they have a better chance of growing up and breeding.

CHANGING SEX

Sexual reproduction requires a male sex cell (sperm) to fuse with a female one (ovum, or egg). Generally, an animal can only produce either male or female sex cells. The bluehead wrasse does things differently. A young female lives with other females and a large, mature "supermale" with a bright blue head. When this male dies, the largest adult female in the group changes sex to become the next supermale.

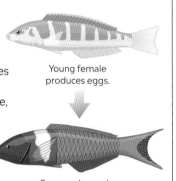

Young female produces eggs.

Supermale produces sperm instead of eggs.

Mothered by father

Seahorses have a unique breeding system—the female produces the eggs and transfers them to a brood pouch on the male's belly. The eggs hatch inside the pouch, but the young, called fry, stay for a while longer, while they adapt to the salty conditions of sea water outside the pouch.

Pouch holds around 200 fry.

Jane Goodall
British zoologist Jane Goodall has studied wild chimpanzees for 60 years. She observed that they show complex social behavior, and that mothers and their young form close bonds. Goodall travels around the world to raise awareness about their protection.

Starter home

Most mammal babies develop inside their mother's womb, or uterus, where a structure called the placenta supplies them with oxygen and food. However, marsupial mammals, such as this kangaroo, give birth to tiny, undeveloped offspring. This young kangaroo (left), called a joey, will complete its development inside the mother's pouch.

Marsupium (pouch)

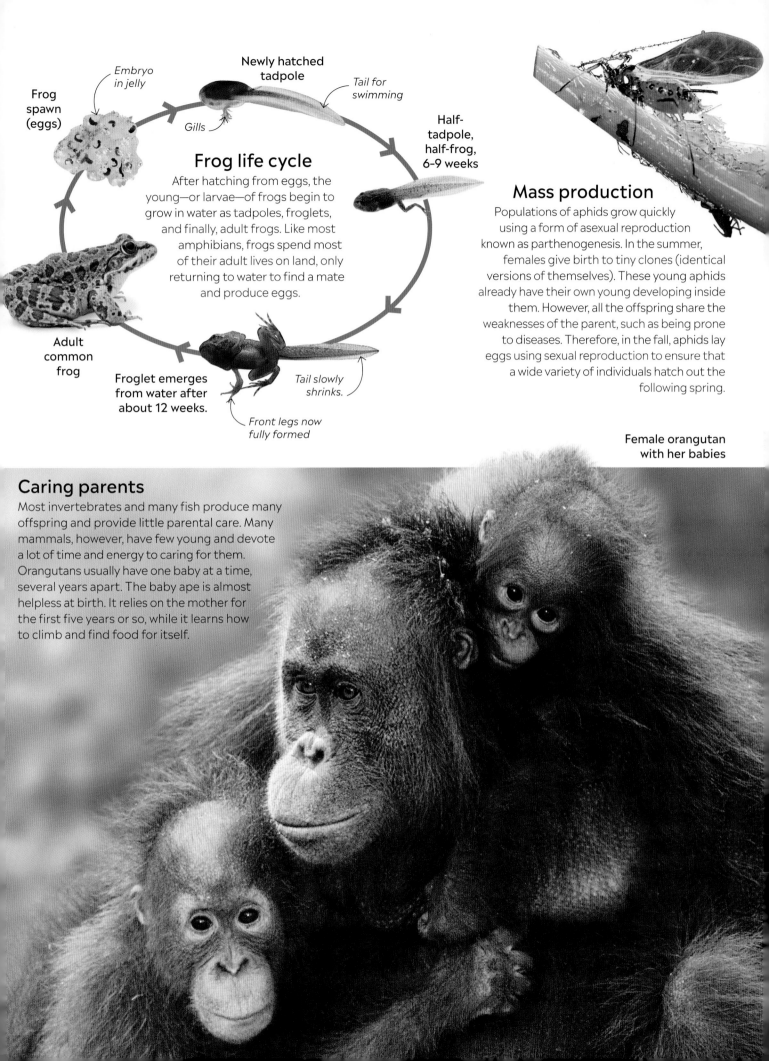

Frog life cycle

Frog spawn (eggs)

Embryo in jelly

Newly hatched tadpole

Tail for swimming

Gills

Half-tadpole, half-frog, 6–9 weeks

After hatching from eggs, the young—or larvae—of frogs begin to grow in water as tadpoles, froglets, and finally, adult frogs. Like most amphibians, frogs spend most of their adult lives on land, only returning to water to find a mate and produce eggs.

Adult common frog

Froglet emerges from water after about 12 weeks.

Tail slowly shrinks.

Front legs now fully formed

Mass production

Populations of aphids grow quickly using a form of asexual reproduction known as parthenogenesis. In the summer, females give birth to tiny clones (identical versions of themselves). These young aphids already have their own young developing inside them. However, all the offspring share the weaknesses of the parent, such as being prone to diseases. Therefore, in the fall, aphids lay eggs using sexual reproduction to ensure that a wide variety of individuals hatch out the following spring.

Female orangutan with her babies

Caring parents

Most invertebrates and many fish produce many offspring and provide little parental care. Many mammals, however, have few young and devote a lot of time and energy to caring for them. Orangutans usually have one baby at a time, several years apart. The baby ape is almost helpless at birth. It relies on the mother for the first five years or so, while it learns how to climb and find food for itself.

Waders, such as these red knots, feed on small animals hiding in the mud.

Marine animals

Life began in the oceans more than 3.5 billion years ago, and the oceans are still home to almost all the major animal groups. However, the oceans are not a single habitat. Marine environments are as different as rocky shores, mangrove swamps, and deep ocean trenches. Even in the open ocean there are variations in temperature, pressure, and saltiness that impact life.

On the shore
The shoreline is a crowded habitat. Here, tides sweep regularly over the shore. When the tides recede, many animals hide out in the mud.

Mantle (body covering)

Fin

Devil in the dark
The deep-sea vampire squid spends its life in constant darkness, but its body produces light—a phenomenon called bioluminescence. The squid flashes its light to lure prey and attract mates. If this attracts predators, it covers the light with its webbed tentacles.

Webbed tentacle

Underwater jungles
Corals are colonies of organisms that are tiny relatives of jellyfish. Each animal is called a polyp and grows a protective case, which is left behind when it dies. Generations of these skeletons build up into limestone reefs that provide different niches for animals, such as these yellow butterfly fish, to live in.

Going flat
A young flounder swims upright, but as it grows, its skull twists so the right eye moves to the left side of the head. With both eyes on the same side of the head, it can look for prey while lying camouflaged on the sea bed.

A docile shark
There are about 500 species of shark. Some are fearsome, sharp-toothed predators, but most are harmless. This bullhead shark uses its sturdy fins to walk across the seabed at night, searching for urchins and crabs to feed on.

Spotted skin camouflages shark against sea bed.

Coastal raiders
Many sea mammals and birds live on the coast but raid the water for food. Terns snatch fish, seals chase down squid, and diving otters collect shellfish. Sea otters have highly buoyant bodies, which is partly due to their thick fur. With 1 million strands of hair per sq in (150,000 strands per sq cm), the fur traps a lot of air.

Schooling
There are few places to hide in the open ocean and some fish swim in clusters called schools, or shoals, to stay safe from predators. Each fish here is darting about, trying to get into the middle of a shoal where it is safer.

Freshwater living

Inland water habitats can be as challenging to life as the oceans. Many aquatic (water-living) animals rely on unpredictable little streams and ponds, which may freeze in winter and dry out in summer. Slow-flowing water loses oxygen, and fish cannot use their gills effectively, while fast-flowing streams are a difficult environment to live in. In addition, animal body tissues, which are full of salts, pull water in from fresh water, so freshwater animals must constantly produce watery urine to flush it out.

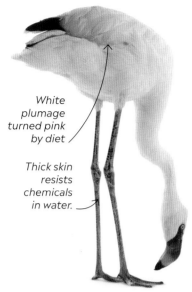

White plumage turned pink by diet

Thick skin resists chemicals in water.

Mineral rich

Not every inland body of water is fresh. Some flamingos live in desert lakes filled with salts and other chemicals. They survive by feeding on tough brine shrimps, which live on a diet of bacteria (small single-celled organisms).

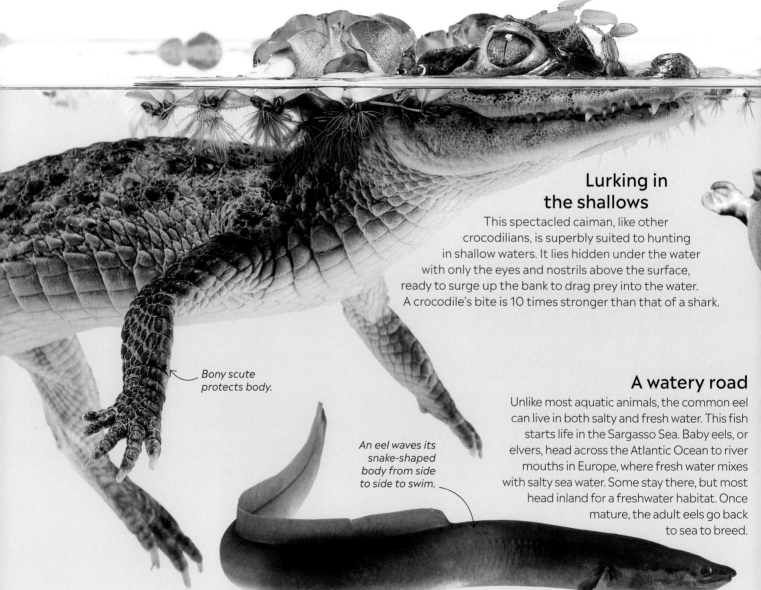

Bony scute protects body.

An eel waves its snake-shaped body from side to side to swim.

Lurking in the shallows

This spectacled caiman, like other crocodilians, is superbly suited to hunting in shallow waters. It lies hidden under the water with only the eyes and nostrils above the surface, ready to surge up the bank to drag prey into the water. A crocodile's bite is 10 times stronger than that of a shark.

A watery road

Unlike most aquatic animals, the common eel can live in both salty and fresh water. This fish starts life in the Sargasso Sea. Baby eels, or elvers, head across the Atlantic Ocean to river mouths in Europe, where fresh water mixes with salty sea water. Some stay there, but most head inland for a freshwater habitat. Once mature, the adult eels go back to sea to breed.

Spider falls from leaf after being hit by water.

Survivors

Tardigrades, or water bears, are microscopic animals that live in all types of water—from hot springs to muddy puddles—and graze on bacteria. They are the toughest creatures alive. When the water dries out or becomes too salty, a tardigrade hauls up its eight legs and becomes dormant for up to 30 years. Scientists have found that tardigrades can even survive in space.

Tree ponds

Freshwater habitats can be found in unusual places. The leaves of succulent jungle plants called bromeliads form a cup that collects rainwater. These little ponds, high up in the trees, are used by many poison dart frogs to raise their young.

Stream of droplets

Water cannon

The archerfish uses water as a weapon. It pokes its lips above the surface, and fires a jet of water out of its mouth with a quick squeeze of its gill covers. The jet can travel up to 10 ft (3 m) into the air, knocking its prey from overhanging leaves into the water.

More than **150,000** species of **animals** make their **home** in **fresh water**.

On their own

Freshwater lakes are isolated habitats with unique wildlife. Lake Baikal, the world's largest lake, in eastern Russia, is home to the only freshwater species of seal, known as the nerpa (above). The ancestors of the nerpa swam upriver from the sea about 80,000 years ago, but the route back to the ocean has since disappeared.

Wet nursery

Many insects, such as the hawker dragonfly, start life in fresh water. This young dragonfly—known as a naiad—uses a sharp mouthpart to spear prey with lightning speed. After months of hunting in shallow pools, the naiad climbs up the stalk of a water plant and transforms into an adult.

Hawker naiad spears a stickleback fish.

Cold and ice

The coldest habitats on Earth are near the Poles, where summers are too short to provide much warmth, and high up on mountains, where the air is too thin to retain heat. Most of the animals that live in cold places are warm-blooded, though some cold-blooded species have evolved adaptations to survive here as well. Some insects can freeze in winter, but still be alive when they thaw out in spring.

High fliers

Bar-headed geese are some of the highest flying birds. They cross over the Himalayas while migrating from the wetlands in India to the Tibetan plateau. The temperature can drop to –22°F (–30°C), and the air is so thin that the geese breathe hundreds of times a minute to get enough oxygen.

Big is best

The bodies of large animals lose heat slowly in cold conditions, which is why animals in cold regions tend to be larger than those in warmer ones. The world's largest deer, the moose, lives in the cold north, as does the gyrfalcon, the biggest falcon. Polar animals also tend to have shorter legs, ears, and tails, which also helps reduce heat loss.

Antarctic krill

Found in plenty

The polar oceans are so cold that the surface of the water freezes over at times. The conditions under the water are less severe, however, and the polar seas thrive with life. In the Southern Ocean in the Antarctic, krill (tiny relatives of shrimp) swarm in their millions, providing an important food source for marine life.

Life in the Arctic

Earth's polar regions experience extreme seasonal changes. Most polar bears are active throughout the year, but pregnant females enter a hibernation-like state and sleep through the winter. Bear cubs are born at this time, growing strong on their mother's milk while she sleeps. Mother and cubs are ready to hunt as soon as summer arrives.

Wide feet do not sink into snow and help make bears strong swimmers.

Wing is larger than those of other geese.

Best foot forward

Mountain goats live on steep cliffs, where only the most sure-footed animals can survive. A mountain goat's hoof has two parts, which spread apart and grab the rough ground like a pincer. The rim of the hoof digs into the ice, helping to grip the surface, while the base is covered in a spongy pad that prevents the animal from slipping.

Hoof has two spread-out toes, which help with balance.

Happy feet

Body heat can cause problems in freezing conditions. Warm skin melts ice, but the ice freezes again almost instantly, bonding it to the skin. Warm blood pumping into the feet loses heat to cold blood flowing back to the heart, so the feet stay cold and never get warm enough to melt the ice.

Penguin chick sits on the father's feet to stay off cold ice.

Iceberg ahead

A beluga whale lives along the edge of the Arctic sea ice. Its white skin provides camouflage among the floating icebergs and helps it hide from orcas and polar bears. The beluga is hairless and keeps warm thanks to a 4-in- (10-cm-) thick layer of fatty blubber under its skin.

Small ear reduces heat loss.

In the **desert**

About one-fifth of Earth's land is very dry and receives less than 10 in (250 mm) of rain in a year. These regions are deserts, and range from the Sahara and other hot, tropical deserts to cold deserts, such as the Gobi in central Asia. Desert animals must cope with high and low temperatures, and go for periods without food or drink.

Swimming in the sand
A sandfish is actually a specialized skink—a type of lizard. Its strong, cylindrical body and short legs help it slither through loose sand. The creature hunts by detecting tiny vibrations made by insects.

Bactrian camel has two humps.

Fat reserves
Water drains quickly through sandy desert soil, so there are few places where plants can grow. Browsers, such as this Bactrian camel of central Asia, can go without water for 10 days and survive on the toughest desert shrubs. The camel carries a supply of food in its humps, in the form of oily fats.

Wing cases are fused shut, stopping body from drying out.

Drinking the fog
The huge sand dunes of Africa's Namib Desert rise up on the coast of the Atlantic Ocean. While rainfall is rare, dense banks of fog often roll in from the sea. Fog-basking beetles sit at the top of the dunes and literally drink the mist. Each beetle does a handstand, and tiny droplets condense on its body, running down grooves that lead to its mouth.

Following the rain

The Arabian oryx, a type of antelope, goes for weeks without drinking, getting water from the plants it feeds on. It can smell rain from miles away, and travels toward fresh plants that grow after rainfall.

Surviving the heat

Frogs need to stay moist in the desert heat. The Australian water-holding frog keeps damp by digging deep into the ground and cocooning itself in a bag of mucus. The cocoon hardens into a barrier that locks in water around the frog's body. The frog can stay underground for years until it rains again.

Without water

Many desert animals, such as this Merriam's kangaroo rat, are active at night to avoid the hot sun. This rodent is the only mammal that can go without drinking for its whole life, getting all the water it needs from its diet of seeds.

KEEPING COOL

Large mammals can get very hot in direct sunlight. Their body temperature can rise above 105.8°F (41°C) to levels that would damage the brain of many mammals. The gazelle has a cooling system that chills the blood entering its brain. This allows the gazelle to keep on running when being chased, while its pursuer must stop to avoid overheating.

Gazelle's brain-cooling system

Some warm blood reaches brain directly.

Cooled blood travels to rest of body.

Blood in network of thin vessels is cooled by air.

Sinus (chamber) filled with cooled blood

Warm blood to brain passes through cool sinus.

Water in fog condenses on beetle's cold body.

Fill the tank

Sandgrouse live in the dry parts of Europe, Africa, and Asia. They are seed eaters, and flock to deserts when flowering plants are in seed. Adult birds fly great distances to find watering holes. They soak their belly feathers to airlift water back to their chicks.

Open grassland

Grasslands grow in areas that are too dry for forests to flourish, but not dry enough for deserts to form. There is enough rain for fast-growing grasses to grow, which provide enough food for the animals that live there. There are no specific food sources to defend, so plant-eating animals frequently stay on the move to find the lushest leaves and grasses.

Pronghorn, a North American, hoofed, grassland mammal

Follow the herd

Large herbivores, such as these wildebeest, gather in herds because it is safer for them to stay together. Every herd member looks out for danger, and when one reacts to a threat, the others follow suit. Predators usually pick off the weaker animals on the edges of a herd. Grazers form the biggest herds on the grassy plains.

Need for speed

There are no places to hide on grasslands, so when danger appears, hoofed animals, such as antelopes and pronghorns, run fast. The pronghorn is capable of reaching speeds of up to 60 mph (100 kph). Hoofed animals run on their tiptoes. Their long feet help them lengthen their legs and increase their stride.

Servals have oval ears with distinct white spots.

Night hunter

It is too easy to be spotted by prey during daylight, so many grassland predators spend their days lazing in the shade, waiting until dark. The serval, an African cat about twice the size of a house cat, uses its large ears to listen for rodents in the grass.

Glass lizard

This reptile is not a snake, but a Pallas's glass lizard, which lives in European and Asian grasslands. It is named the glass lizard because it appears to break in two, like a piece of brittle glass, when picked up by the tail.

Silent stalker

Unlike other birds of prey that swoop over grasslands, the secretary bird hunts on foot. Stalking slowly through short grass, this gangly bird watches the ground intently, and when a small animal comes out from a hiding place, it traps the prey with its foot. The bird then uses its hooked beak to kill the victim.

Nesting underground

Temperate (cool) grasslands, such as the American prairies, have almost no trees at all. The American burrowing owl, therefore, nests underground. It usually does not dig the den, but sets up home in a hole vacated by another burrowing animal, such as a prairie dog. The burrow provides the owl with a shelter from predators.

Termites

The most important grazers (grass eaters) in some grasslands are tiny insects called termites. Like an ant's nest, a termite colony has a queen, but unlike an ant's nest, it also has a king. Millions of termites live in tall mounds, made of mud reinforced with dried grass. A natural cooling system reduces the heat produced by the termites.

Ventilation shaft

Chimney lets out rising hot air.

Fungus grows on heaps of grass cuttings and provides food for nymphs.

Worker termite

Nursery chamber houses nymphs (young termites).

Queen lives in a royal chamber.

Underground cellar draws in cool air from outside mound.

Among the trees

More animals are found in forests than in any other habitat. Forests range from hot, damp jungles to cold conifer woodlands in the far north. A single tropical rainforest tree can house more than a thousand species. In all cases, the tall trees provide hundreds of different habitats.

Foraging on the floor

Most of the time, this giant millipede remains hidden among leaf litter—the thick layer of dead leaves that covers the floor of a forest. It grazes on dead plant material on the forest floor.

Fruits and nuts

This toucan is a frugivore (fruit eater). The bird's colorful bill is long enough to reach fruits dangling from flimsy branches, and its jagged edge is strong enough to crack open nuts.

Cuvier's toucan

EYEWITNESS

Justin Sather

Teenager Justin Sather's love of frogs inspired him to work for their protection. As part of the conservation group Reserva: The Youth Land Trust, he has raised enough money to protect 100 acres of rainforest in Ecuador—home to some of the rarest frogs in the world.

Target in sight

The vine snake has a groove that runs from each eye to the tip of its snout that works like a gun sight. The snake lines up the grooves to zero in on mice and small birds.

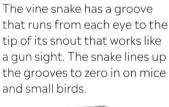

Hidden away

In the dappled light of the forest, a jaguar's distinctive pattern of blotchy rosettes (roselike markings) makes for perfect camouflage. This helps the predator hide in the foliage and sneak up on deer and other prey.

Up the tree

Moisture-loving frogs can easily survive high up in the branches of rainforests. Tree frogs crawl along leaves, using suckers on their toes to grip flat surfaces. If this nocturnal red-eyed tree frog is threatened by a predator, the frog stares squarely at it and flashes its startling body colors.

Vertical pupil tracks moving insects.

Getting noticed

Sometimes animals need to get noticed to attract mates. When resting with its wings folded, the blue morpho butterfly may look drab among the leaves. However, when it flies, its shimmering blue wings are revealed.

Hanging out

When living so high up, just one foot out of place could be fatal. The New World monkeys of South America get a helping hand from their prehensile tail, which can wrap around a branch. The tail has a hairless pad at the tip that also aids grip.

MANY LEVELS

Tropical rainforests have layers that function as habitats for different groups of animals. At the top are occasional giant trees called emergents. They and the canopy trees are out in the sunshine, but they block out the light, making the forest floor a gloomy place. The canopy forms a continuous layer that is home to most rainforest animals.

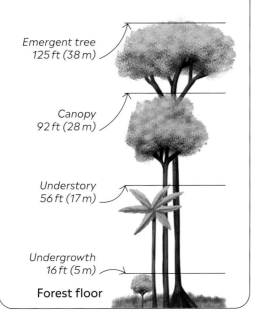

Emergent tree 125 ft (38 m)

Canopy 92 ft (28 m)

Understory 56 ft (17 m)

Undergrowth 16 ft (5 m)

Forest floor

The right fit

Jungle mammals tend to be smaller than those living in open habitats. Being smaller helps this African forest elephant when pushing through thick foliage. Jungle birds, on the other hand, appear to have longer bills, or beaks, than their relatives in cooler places. The large beak might act as a radiator to give out heat, so the birds' bodies do not overheat.

Taking to **the air**

In the history of life on Earth, four distinct groups of animal—insects, pterosaurs (flying reptiles), birds, and bats—evolved adaptations that enabled flight. Today, each flying animal combines a light body weight with high muscle power. It is lifted off the ground by wings. As the wings cut through the air, they create a lift force that opposes gravity, and raises the animal in the air.

Long fifth finger supports wing of skin.

Pterodactylus

Flying reptiles
The first flying vertebrates were the pterosaurs. These reptiles became extinct at the same time as their dinosaur relatives. One of the first fossil pterosaurs discovered was *Pterodactylus*, meaning "wing finger"—its wing was mostly skin stretched behind a single finger bone.

Handy wings
Bats are the only mammals that can fly. Although they can see, many bats use echolocation to find their way—they emit high-pitched chirps that echo from objects around them. Based on the echoes, they figure out the distances to the objects, forming a sound picture of their surroundings.

Skin stretches between finger bones.

Secondary flight feather

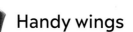

Wing is a thin membrane running between stiff veins.

The wing twists as it moves up, cutting through the air, but flattens again as it flaps down, pushing against the air.

The wing is powered by muscles at its base.

Four wings first
Insects were the first animals to fly. No other invertebrate group has taken to the air since. It is believed that the first flying insects, which appeared around 350 million years ago, had four wings and looked like today's dragonflies. Insect wings are not modified legs, like those of birds and bats, and may have evolved from gills of aquatic larvae.

The back wing moves in opposite direction to front wings in slow flight, to reduce speed while continuing to provide the lifting force for flight.

Staying put

Hummingbirds use their long feathery tongues to lap nectar from delicate flowers while hovering in mid-air. The birds beat their wings up to 70 times a second to hover, making the wings look like a blur. To beat this fast, they have very flexible triangular wings, but such wings are not well suited for flying long distances.

Dinosaurs were the first animals to evolve feathers, around 235 million years ago.

Toe is very long and supports large "parachute" area.

Falling not flying

Wallace's flying frog lives high in the trees of Southeast Asia's jungles. It leaps into the air to escape predators and to reach mates in pools on the forest floor. The frog's large webbed feet break its fall like a parachute, but this is not the same as flying.

Neck vertebra (neck bone)

Humerus (upper arm bone)

Pollex (thumb bone)

Finger bone

Radius (a lower arm bone)

Metacarpal (fused hand bone)

Backbone

Hip bone

Ulna (a lower arm bone)

Masters of the air

Birds are the most varied and widespread flying animals. Different birds have different wing shapes that enable many kinds of flying style. For example, this heron has broad wings that allow slow gliding, while a swift's pointed wings let it swoop at high speed. A bird's bones are thin, hollow, and lightweight—a third of its body weight is in the strong flight muscles in its plump breast.

Tail feather

Forewing has a black patch with a white bar.

Tibia (shin bone)

Ankle

Skeleton of gray heron

Epic journey

Some butterflies migrate long distances. A painted lady butterfly (right) travels 9,000 miles (14,000 km) on its annual migration from tropical Africa to the Arctic, breeding along the route. A butterfly's life is short and the journey is very long, which means that none of the butterflies that leave Africa reach the Arctic—only their descendants arrive.

Toe bone

Small eyespots

Animal homes

Some animals are always on the move, searching for food and mates. Others live in one area, defending their territory from intruders. Still others set up temporary homes to hibernate or raise their young. A bird's nest is perhaps the best known example of an animal's home, but even large mammals, such as gorillas, build nests.

Stitched homes

Male masked weaver birds knit grass to build nests, and then they invite female weavers to inspect their work. If a female likes a nest, she pairs with its builder because she considers him a good mate with whom to raise chicks.

1 Best location

The male first chooses a small branch for the nest near the tops of trees, out of reach of climbing predators, such as snakes.

House of leaves

Weaver ants live in trees. Teams of worker ants haul the edges of leaves together, while other adults bind the leaves together with a sticky silk, produced by larvae. Adults hold larvae like tubes of glue to form a boxlike nest.

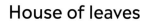

Silk produced by ant larvae glues together edges of leaves.

Diving bell

A water spider's web is not a sticky fly trap. Instead, it holds the spider's air supply during hunting dives. The spider retreats to its bubble home to digest food. Its web works like a gill, releasing carbon dioxide and taking in oxygen from the water.

Case made from plant stems and pebbles

Front end enlarges as larva grows inside.

A bits-and-pieces home

Caddis fly larvae live in freshwater streams. Some species weave a silk tube to live in, which acts as a net to catch specks of food. Other caddis flies use their silk to glue bits of the riverbed into an armored case. This case (left) is open at both ends.

2 In the loop

The nest starts out as a single loop of woven grasses and twigs. The bird adds more loops to build up the spherical shape of the nest.

Fresh, flexible stalks are easier to weave.

Size of spherical nest depends on the bird's reach.

3 Make or break

If a female likes the nest, she lines it with grass and feathers. If no female likes it, the male weaver breaks it apart.

Hanging homes

Bats roost in high places, crawling into rocky crevices or clinging onto high tree branches surrounded by leaves. This horseshoe bat hangs from the roof of a cave by its back legs. Its toes have a locking mechanism that grips tighter as the foot muscles are relaxed.

Entrance at bottom of nest

Marking territory

This otter is marking its territory, leaving smelly droppings as scent marks—a sign that it controls the area. The otter finds its food within its territory and ensures that others stay away. When an otter smells another otter's scent, it knows an intruder is around.

Otters have scent glands all over their body.

Hermit crabs make their home in the discarded shells of other animals.

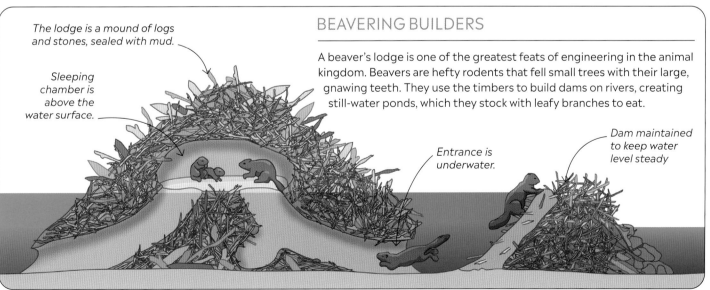

BEAVERING BUILDERS

A beaver's lodge is one of the greatest feats of engineering in the animal kingdom. Beavers are hefty rodents that fell small trees with their large, gnawing teeth. They use the timbers to build dams on rivers, creating still-water ponds, which they stock with leafy branches to eat.

The lodge is a mound of logs and stones, sealed with mud.

Sleeping chamber is above the water surface.

Entrance is underwater.

Dam maintained to keep water level steady

Migrations

A migration is a journey that an animal undertakes, often along a set route. It is neither an aimless search for food nor simply patrolling territory. A migration has start and end points, and the animal always makes a return journey, or its descendants do. Animals migrate in response to changes in the seasons, which make it hard for them to survive.

Birthing site

Humpback whales spend the summer in the rich feeding grounds of polar seas. However, this water is too cold for newborn calves. Therefore, in winter, these whales migrate to warmer seas near the equator to give birth. The calves then return to colder waters with their mothers.

Birds take turns to lead the flock.

Martin Wikelski
German ornithologist Martin Wikelski is an expert in animal migration. By attaching radio transmitters to migrating birds, he can collect satellite data on the birds' direction of travel, speed, and any stops they make on the way.

Following the stream

The life cycle of each of these colorful sockeye salmon is one long migration. The fish start out in the headwaters of a river. As they grow, they head downstream, finally reaching the sea, where they mature over several years. The adult salmon travel all the way upriver to their birthplace to spawn, after which they die.

North bound

Snow geese fly north from warm New Mexico to the Arctic tundra, which is frozen for most of the year. They time their arrival with the summer thaw, when insects swarm around boggy pools. The geese nest in the melting landscape, feeding the bugs to their chicks.

Walking the ocean

These spiny lobsters march across the Caribbean sea bed during their fall migration to warmer waters. The lobsters also head for deeper waters, perhaps to escape the storms that disrupt their shallow summer territory.

Antennae rubbing makes rasping noises that frighten attackers.

STAYING ON COURSE

Most migratory animals first learn a route by following their parents. Later, they rely on many clues to find their way, such as following winds or ocean currents, tracking Earth's magnetic field, or remembering landmarks. Some know the way instinctively—it is coded in their genes. Migratory routes often have places to rest and, generally, they avoid difficult obstacles. Arctic terns have the longest route of all.

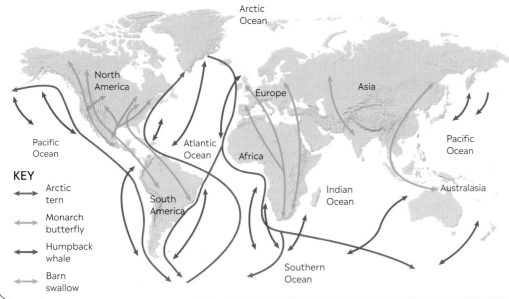

KEY

- ⟷ Arctic tern
- ⟷ Monarch butterfly
- ⟷ Humpback whale
- ⟷ Barn swallow

Mountain meeting

Monarch butterflies are one of the few insects to migrate. Every fall in North America, millions of them fly south—around 2,800 miles (4,500 km). The butterflies crowd into some mountain forests in Mexico to escape the winter, before heading north again in spring.

Staying alive

In the wild, animals face a constant struggle for survival. Predators must kill prey for food, while prey must always be ready to fend off a predator's attack. Both predator and prey are in a race to stay a step ahead of each other, each animal adapting constantly in the presence of an evolving foe.

Hidden trickster

The Peringuey's adder lives in the deserts of southwest Africa. This snake is not easy to spot—its rough scales match the sand and it lies waiting to ambush prey, such as this gecko. The snake lures the lizard within biting distance by wiggling the dark tip of its tail.

Mimics

This owl butterfly would make an easy meal for a rainforest tree frog. But the hungry frog stays away from it because when the butterfly opens its wings, two dark spots suddenly appear. This fools the frog into believing that it is looking into the eyes of a dangerous owl.

Traps of silk

The ogre-faced spider eats insects, which scuttle for safety at the slightest scare. So this spider hangs motionless just above the ground, flexing a sticky net in its four front legs. It waits for prey to walk under the net, then moves with lightning speed to snare it.

BUBBLE NETS

For humpback whales, eating a few fish at a time takes far too long to fill their stomachs. So they band together to herd fish into tight shoals that are perfect for eating in gulps. The whales swim in a spiral, blowing a curtain of bubbles, and making the fish crowd together at the surface. Then, they surge up from below with their mouths gaping open.

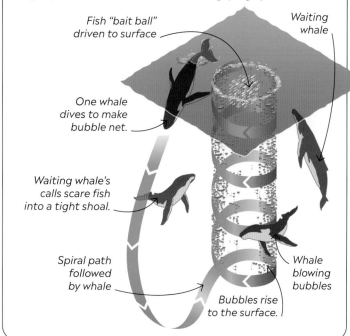

Fish "bait ball" driven to surface

Waiting whale

One whale dives to make bubble net.

Waiting whale's calls scare fish into a tight shoal.

Spiral path followed by whale

Whale blowing bubbles

Bubbles rise to the surface.

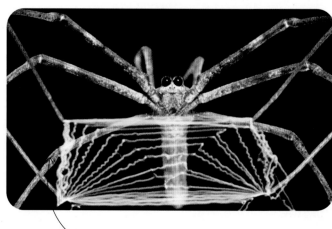

Dry outer strand is held by spider.

Tail regrows slowly.

Two lives

If grabbed by the tail, the tree skink snaps it off to escape. The predator is left with a wriggling detached tail. The skink regenerates a new tail, but this one does not detach in the next attack.

Diving down

A kingfisher has evolved eyes that allow it to spot fish before entering water. Water bends light, so the bird has to adjust its eyes when targeting underwater prey. The bird's spear-shaped beak and streamlined body help it punch through the water easily as it dives for fish.

Spraying acid

In any colony, only the queen ant produces young, so it is common for worker ants to sacrifice themselves to protect her. To ward off predators, wood ants employ chemical weapons. They squirt formic acid from their abdomens— the same chemical that causes the burning pain of a bee sting.

👁 EYEWITNESS

Alan McFadyen
Scottish wildlife photographer Alan McFadyen spent six years trying to capture the exact moment when a kingfisher hits the surface of water in search of fish (left). He took an amazing 720,000 pictures before achieving the perfect shot.

45

Living together

Animals frequently rely on another animal species for their survival. Such a link is called symbiosis, which means "together living" in ancient Greek. There are three kinds of symbiosis. In parasitism, only one species benefits from the relationship, while the other—known as the host—is weakened by it. Mutualism is a relationship in which both species benefit, while in commensalism one animal benefits, while the other is unaffected.

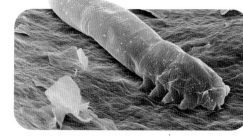

Tiny passenger

About 50 percent of people live in symbiosis with this microscopic eyelash mite. It lives in the follicle (a small sac or cavity from which a hair grows) of the human eyelash, eating oily skin flakes.

Plaintive cuckoo chick

Cuckoo in the nest

This cuckoo chick is being fed by a male sunbird. The chick's mother laid the egg in the sunbird's nest. The cuckoo is a brood parasite—an animal that tricks another into raising its young. A cuckoo's egg looks a lot like a sunbird egg, so the sunbird fails to spot the interloper. Once the chick hatches, it ejects any sunbird chicks or unhatched eggs.

Wingless aphid sucks sap constantly.

Aphid farms

Aphids are insects that drink plant sap. With a purely liquid diet, the little aphids produce a lot of sugary urine, known as honeydew. Some ants will stand guard over a herd of aphids, keeping away predators. The ants "milk" the aphids, stroking them to make them produce sweet droplets of honeydew. This relationship is an example of mutualism.

Male mariqua sunbird

Pecking to order

The red-billed oxpecker lives among the herds of grazing mammals, such as this zebra, that roam across the grasslands of Africa. It slides its flat beak between the hairs of the host to pluck ticks and lice from its host's skin. The zebra gets a cleaning service, while the bird is rewarded with tasty, blood-sucking parasites. The oxpecker may also act as a parasite, feeding on blood from open wounds.

The big eyes of a watchman goby give it good eyesight.

Teaming up

The watchman goby and the pistol shrimp team up on the sandy sea bed. The shrimp digs a burrow, while the fish acts as the shrimp's lookout. If danger approaches, the goby flicks the shrimp with its tail, and the duo dash inside.

Short-sighted shrimp keeps the burrow clean.

Ridged sucker is formed from a flattened dorsal fin.

Remora

Hyena stands over its food in a defensive posture.

Thieving carnivores

Hyenas are skilled hunters that can take prey as large as zebra, but they will also steal and feast on carcasses killed by other carnivores. This behavior is called kleptoparasitism. But the hyena's meal is not safe either—other thieves may try to snatch a bite.

Free meals

Commensalism is rare compared to the other forms of symbiosis. The remora sticks itself to large sharks using a sucker on the top of its head. The fish eats its host's droppings or the leftovers from the host's meals.

Black-backed jackal—another kleptoparasite— is wary of the hyena.

Living in groups

Humans are not the only animals that live in societies. There are advantages and disadvantages to being a social animal. Group members have to share many things, such as food. Adult males may also have to compete for the same females in the group. Despite these problems, the members of a group stick together. In all cases, animal societies function as a delicate balance where the gains outweigh the losses.

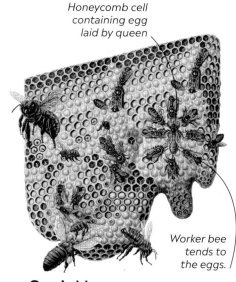

Honeycomb cell containing egg laid by queen

Worker bee tends to the eggs.

Social bees

Honeybees have an advanced level of social organization that is also seen in ants, termites, and some wasps. A single female—the queen bee—produces the offspring. The rest of the society is made up of female worker bees and male drones, who fly off to mate with young queens.

Fisher's lovebirds

Pairing up

The smallest animal group is a breeding pair. In lovebirds—a small species of parrot—a male and a female pair up for life. Even if the two birds spend long periods apart, they meet up and raise chicks together when the breeding season comes. This single-mate system is called monogamy.

Superpods at sea

Dolphins and whales live in family groups called pods, which typically contain about 15 animals. When several pods converge at one place to feed, a superpod forms.

Rank and file

Hamadryas baboons of East Africa and Arabia live in a highly ordered society. In a troop of around 100, every monkey has a rank. Big adult males take the lead over a group of females, and several of these groups band together as a clan—one of many per troop. Males frequently fight over females—young males are always ready to take over from an older male—but if a low-ranking monkey steps out of line, it is punished with a bite.

Dominant male has tufts of gray fur.

Baby travels with its mother.

Young male is not allowed to mate.

Female may be stolen by another group.

Hunting in a team

The wolf is one of the few animals that can kill prey that is bigger than it is. It does this by working in a team, or pack. Wolves can follow prey for hours on end without getting tired, so the pack chases prey, taking turns to bite their victim until it crashes to the ground.

Wolves howl to warn other packs to stay away.

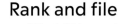

Population explosion

Locust swarms are some of the largest animal groupings, containing billions of insects. These large grasshoppers normally live on their own, but crowd together in search of food.

One of the crowd

Seabirds, such as these gannets, nest together in huge colonies, called rookeries. The parents take turns to dive for food out at sea, bringing some back for the chicks.

The human animal

The human species is called *Homo sapiens* and it belongs to a group of mammals called the primates. The animals most closely related to humans are chimpanzees. These two species share at least 98 percent of their DNA (p.14). However, the remaining bit of DNA is enough to make the two primates very different.

Rounded skull on top of neck

S-shaped spine (backbone) helps absorb shocks while walking.

Barrel-shaped rib cage allows arms to swing, helping the body balance on two legs.

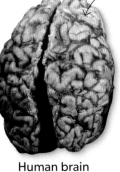 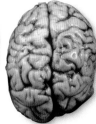
Folds increase space for nerve cells.

Human brain   Gorilla brain

A complex brain
Humans have the largest brain in the animal kingdom, when compared to their body size. It is much larger than the brain of a gorilla—a close relative—and has 120 billion nerve cells.

Using medicine
Some mammals, such as dogs and chimpanzees, eat certain plants when they feel unwell. This is called self-medication—something that humans also do. Many cultures have used willow and meadowsweet to make painkilling drinks. Humans isolate products from plants to make medicines and treat illnesses.

Painkilling tablets   Meadowsweet

Wide pelvis cradles and supports the soft organs.

On two legs
These skeletons highlight some of the anatomical differences between humans and gorillas. Gorillas walk mostly on all fours. Humans, however, are bipedal—mammals that walk upright on two feet. This mode of locomotion frees the hands and helps them see long distances.

Thigh bones are angled inward toward knees keeping upper body over the hips.

Farmer working in rice field

Growing food
Early humans ate what they could find, killing some animals, but surviving mainly on seeds, roots, and fruits. About 10,000 years ago, humans learned to grow food plants, such as rice and wheat, and this was the birth of farming.

Heel and toes of foot touch the ground.

Human skeleton

Global animal

Electric lights at night indicate where the human settlements cluster in different areas around the world. Humans evolved in Africa, spreading across Europe, Asia, and Australia about 40,000 years ago, and reaching the Americas around 20,000 years ago. Humans are also the only vertebrates to stay in the frozen Antarctic all year round.

Using tools

Many animals use tools—chimpanzees, for instance, use twigs to collect termites. However, by far the most sophisticated tools are created by humans. These range from stone cutters first used by *Homo habilis* 2.5 million years ago, and metal tools such as this pocket knife, to complex modern tools such as the computer chip and the internal combustion engine.

Adult male has a tall, bony head crest.

Shoulder blades at the back allow a large range of movement.

Cone-shaped rib cage allows arms to swivel above the head.

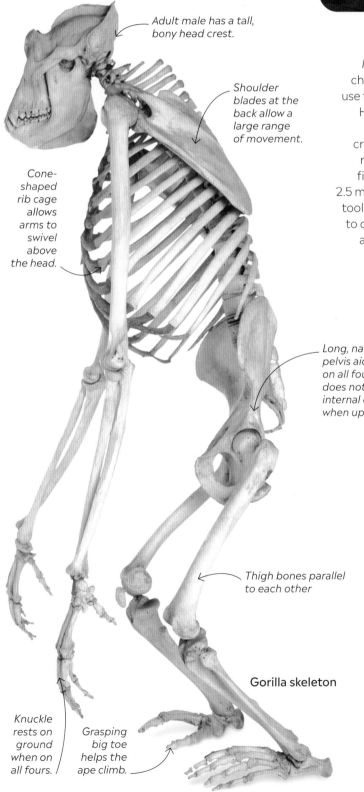

Long, narrow pelvis aids walking on all fours, but does not support internal organs when upright.

Thigh bones parallel to each other

Gorilla skeleton

Knuckle rests on ground when on all fours.

Grasping big toe helps the ape climb.

Modern humans evolved around 150,000 years ago, many million years after chimpanzees.

Living together

Unlike our earliest ancestors who lived in groups of about 150, today most of us live in crowded communities. This has led to humans adopting behaviors that help them live in big groups. For example, human beings are accepting of strangers (unlike chimpanzees), and use spoken language for bonding and communication.

Livestock

Thousands of years ago, humans began to domesticate and rear useful animals, using them for their muscle power, products, and body parts. The first livestock (farm animals) were sheep and goats, which were probably domesticated around 10,000 years ago. Gradually, the list of livestock grew to include cattle, pigs, and chickens.

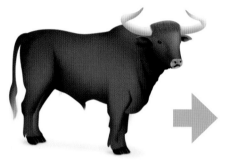
Aurochs—the ancestor of modern cattle

Scottish Aberdeen Angus is bred for good quality meat.

Then and now
The domestic cow is a descendant of an ancient grazer called the aurochs, which lived across Europe and Asia. Zebus (right) are descended from Indian aurochs, while beef cattle are related to European aurochs.

Wild inside
Despite centuries of captive breeding to shape domestic animals into tame and productive creatures, some still exhibit certain wild characteristics. For example, sheep dash uphill when frightened—just as their ancestor, the small and sturdy mouflon, would do when it needed to escape attackers in the rocky mountains of western Asia.

A living ancestor
Every domestic animal is a descendant of a wild ancestor. Many of these wild animals are extinct or very rare. However, red jungle fowl—believed to be the wild form of the chicken—are still widespread in Southeast Asia.

Red jungle fowl cockerel

Woolly jumper

For millennia, humans have used the fur of other mammals to stay warm. Woolly hairs can be spun into yarn, and used to weave warm clothing. Wool comes from sheep, alpacas, camels, and goats. Perhaps the softest hair is found on fluffy angora rabbits.

Bug to dye for

In the 16th century, Spanish colonizers in South America were intrigued by how the local people dyed their clothes deep red. Cochineal bugs, which live on cacti, produce a chemical that is used to make the dye.

Silk Route

The Silk Route—an ancient trade route from China in the East to the Mediterranean in the West—was named after silk, the most lucrative product to be traded along it. Silk is produced by silkworms—moth caterpillars that live on mulberry tree leaves. The silkworms above are kept at a breeding base in Matou town, China.

Zebu are specially bred to have longer, more curved horns than their ancestors.

Animal workers

The first working animals may have been half-tamed wolves who lived alongside humans about 15,000 years ago. These animals barked to warn humans of approaching danger. Before the invention of engines, many machines, such as wheeled carts and water pumps, were powered by animals. Today, humans use many animals for their natural abilities.

Trained **dolphins** use **echolocation** (biological sonar) to detect underwater **mines**.

To the rescue
This search dog uses its great sense of smell to find people buried in snow. A dog's scent-detection is far superior to a human's—a dog's nose contains 195 million more smell receptors than ours.

Tracking device attached to flipper

Animal soldiers
This bottlenose dolphin works for the US Navy. A dolphin's brain is larger than a human's, but not as complex. Nevertheless, the dolphin is highly intelligent, and can be trained to recognize mines in the water. Other navy dolphins are trained to search for injured divers.

Thick skin can withstand extreme temperatures.

Hard worker
A mule's father (sire) is a donkey, and its mother (dam) is a horse. Specially bred to work as beasts of burden, mules are big and strong like a horse, but calm and sure-footed like a donkey.

Truffle hunting

One of the world's most expensive foods, truffles are fungi that grow on the forest floor and are difficult for humans to find. Trained animals, such as dogs, easily track down truffles using their excellent sense of smell. The fungus is then dug up and shipped to restaurants and markets.

Dancing horses

Slovenian Lipizzaner horses are descended from Spanish and North African varieties. They were bred to be strong and agile. Some stallions are trained to dance.

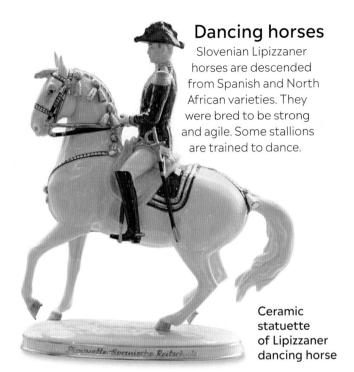

Ceramic statuette of Lipizzaner dancing horse

Easy to study

Scientists use fruit flies from the genus *Drosophila* to study genes. They alter a fly's genetic structure to see how this changes the way the insect grows. Genetic alteration has made this fly grow extra wings. The flies breed quickly, making it easy to study many generations.

Extra pair of wings

Fruit fly with modified genes

Pest controller

The mongoose is a small carnivore that lives in Asia and Africa. Many species are good at killing snakes, and in some countries they are used as pest controllers. A mongoose can tackle even a cobra, one of the most venomous snakes.

Hidden guard

This Pyrenean mountain dog is used to protect sheep from wolves, lynxes, and bears in the mountains between France and Spain. It has been bred to be a "dog in sheep's clothing"—its shaggy white fur helps it mingle with the flock, and the sheep soon grow used to it.

Shaggy white fur

Sheep remain calm in dog's presence.

Animal friends

People often make room in their families for animals kept as companions. The most popular pets are cats and dogs—there are several hundred million of them. People also keep other animals as pets, from deadly snakes to tiny insects.

Border collie catches a toy in the air.

The wolf within

All pet dogs are descended from wild wolves. Dogs and humans are both social species, which makes it easier for them to live together. Wolves began living alongside humans about 15,000 years ago. They scavenged on waste food and, once domesticated, may have teamed up with humans for hunting.

All in the family

Hamsters have pouches in their cheeks that store seeds, a useful feature in these desert rodents which can go for many days without finding food. These pouches give the hamsters cute rounded faces. In the 1930s, hamsters became fashionable pets.

Skin has blue-gray patches.

Mutant creatures

Some breeds of pet are mutants that could not survive in the wild. This strange-looking sphynx cat is descended from a single Canadian cat that was born hairless in 1966. Sphynx cats suffer in cold weather without a covering of hair and would not survive outside a warm house.

Many breeds

Each dog breed has certain characteristics. For example, this border collie is intelligent and can follow instructions from its master. Collies are working dogs, commonly used as sheep dogs. The tiny chihuahua breed is the same species as a collie, but is 10 times smaller and was bred to be easy to carry, pet, and cuddle.

Creepy pets

Some people like to keep dangerous animals as pets. It was once believed that a tarantula's bite was deadly, and produced dangerous convulsions. However, a tarantula's bite is largely harmless to humans.

Winged companions

Parrots are famous for the way they can copy sounds, such as repeating the words people say. Most parrots are too large to keep in a cage, but budgerigars—small Australian parrots (right)—make good pets. Parrots mimic well because, in the wild, they learn a local set of calls by copying older parrots.

Color of feathers is created by selective breeding.

Japanese children play with goldfish.

Fish in a bowl

About 1,000 years ago—probably first in China—people began keeping carp as pets. Over the years, people created eye-catching breeds, such as goldfish and koi, which are now popular around the world. Fish use bright colors to attract mates, and many vibrant species from coral reefs and tropical rivers are also common pets today.

The wild side

The dingo is one of Australia's most widespread animals. It was introduced to the continent about 4,000 years ago when people brought pet dogs over from Southeast Asia. These dogs escaped and became feral (reverted to a wild state). Now, dingoes living in packs are one of Australia's main predators.

Pests

In the wild there is no such thing as a pest, but humans label some animals "pests" when they damage crops, harm domestic animals, or spread diseases. Humans, meanwhile, have a very large impact on the environment—we turn wild land into fields and cities. While most animals lose areas of their habitat in this process, a few species benefit and thrive in these artificial landscapes.

City slackers

The pigeons living in cities are feral—they are descended from domestic pigeons that were once kept for food or for carrying messages. The wild relatives of pigeons are called rock doves, which roost on steep cliffs. City pigeons feed on a diet of waste food, and breed four or five times a year.

Fruit killer

Helix aspersa, or garden snail, is a land snail native to Europe. It is usually seen grazing on leaves in vegetable patches and fruit trees. In the last 150 years, this snail has spread to many other regions of the world by hitching a ride on imported vegetables.

Pest at home

Cockroaches live wherever there is rotting waste, such as leftover food. These pests, which can carry diseases, originally came from humid African jungles, but have set up home in basements and sewers around the world.

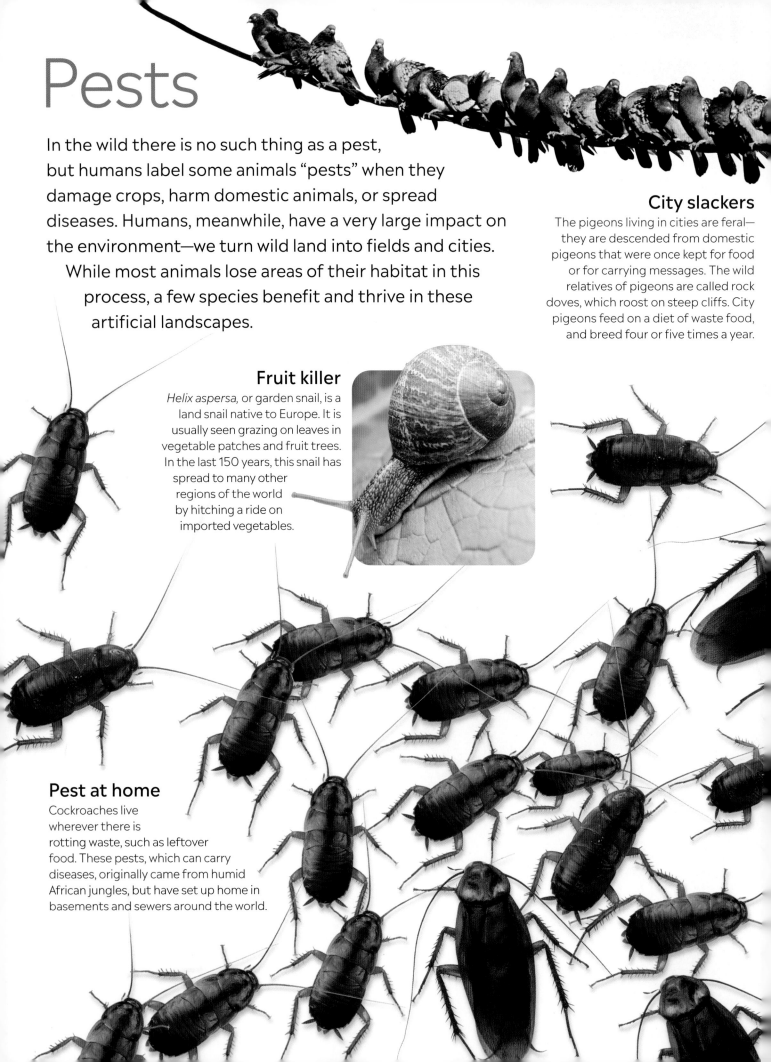

Accidental pest

In the 1930s, giant toads from South America were introduced to Australia, to eat beetles that were ruining sugar cane crops. However, these ground-dwelling toads could not reach the beetles high up in the canes. So they spread out in search of food and ended up becoming pests themselves, preying on local wildlife and carrying diseases.

Deadly bloodsucker

Female mosquitoes drink the blood of humans to get the nutrients they need to grow eggs. When biting, the mosquitoes secrete saliva into the victim's blood. This saliva may carry germs that can cause deadly diseases, such as yellow fever, elephantiasis, and malaria.

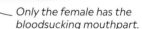

Only the female has the bloodsucking mouthpart.

Making a nuisance

Moles are seldom seen, but the hills of soil they produce when digging fresh tunnels ruin a neat lawn. Moles that dig under trees produce fewer molehills because the tree roots support the burrows.

Small hair on abdomen detects air currents created by an attacker from behind.

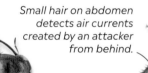

Dummy hunters

Animals become pests when they are taken out of their natural habitats and away from predators that keep their populations in check. However, pests continue to be on the lookout for threats in human settlements. This lifelike model owl keeps crows, mice, and seed-eating birds away from fields and gardens.

Bringer of death

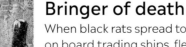

When black rats spread to Europe from Asia on board trading ships, fleas living on the rats carried a disease called the plague. The worst outbreak of plague—termed the Black Death—was in the 14th century, when 100 million people were killed. The last major outbreak of the plague in England was in 1665.

Animals in danger

Human activities and industries can affect animals and their habitats. They may face a shortage of food or places to raise their young, resulting in a drop in their numbers. Protecting the environment is called conservation, and conservationists work hard to preserve natural habitats and the animals that live in them.

Pollution

These fish have died after crude oil was spilled into water, filling it with poisons. This is an example of pollution, which is the presence of harmful substances in the environment. Pollutants are most often chemicals released into water or air from homes or factories, but can also be excessive heat, or loud noises.

The **Arctic ice** could **disappear** by **2040** if Earth continues to heat up at the current rate.

Trade bans

Wild animals are often protected by law. A ban on ivory trading makes it illegal to sell this elephant tusk anywhere in the world. With this ban, the world's governments hoped to reduce the number of elephants killed illegally for their tusks. Since the ban, elephant numbers have been rising.

An elephant tusk is a long incisor tooth.

Habitat loss

Humans can put animals at risk by damaging their habitats. The 'ōhi'a tree was the main provider of the nectar eaten by 'i'iwi birds of Hawai'i. Due to the introduction of new trees by humans, the 'ōhi'a tree is disappearing. These birds must find new food sources to survive.

'I'iwi bird feeding on flowers of an 'ōhi'a tree

Climate impact

Earth's climate is changing rapidly, driven by human activities such as deforestation and burning fossil fuels. Changing weather patterns are making habitats hotter, cooler, wetter, or drier than before, putting many animal species at risk. The golden toad (below) was declared extinct in 2004, because it had not been recorded for 15 years. Its Costa Rican rainforest habitat became hotter and drier, which allowed an invasive fungus to thrive and infect the golden toad population.

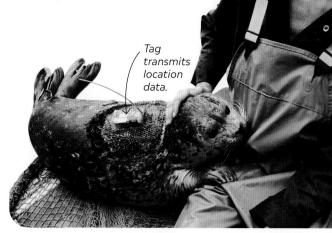

Tag transmits location data.

Studying animals

Sometimes animal numbers decrease without obvious reason. To understand why, scientists gather data about animals and their environment. This harbor seal lives in an area polluted by an oil spill. It has been fitted with a tag that records where the seal hunts for fish, and this helps the experts build up a map of which areas of ocean have recovered and which are still polluted.

Walrus uses its tusks to climb on to ice floe.

Changing fast

In the Arctic Ocean, walruses rest on ice floes (floating ice) after hunting for shellfish on the sea bed. In recent years, the sea ice in the Arctic has decreased due to global warming. As a result, walruses have to rest on the shore, where they are more vulnerable to predators, such as polar bears.

Paying for protection

One way to help protect habitats is through ecotourism, where the money spent by tourists goes back into local conservation projects. In some African national parks, safaris are carefully designed to have minimum impact on wildlife and its environment, while still allowing people to see the animals up close.

👁 EYEWITNESS

Rylee Brooke Kamahele
At the age of 12, Rylee Kamahele fought for legislation to strengthen environmental protection in Hawai'i. This included a reduction in the single use of plastic products and stronger conservation of marine life around her island home.

Animals and myths

Myths and legends often feature animals that can do amazing things, including talking to one another. Mythical monsters can have a basis in the natural world. For example, the phoenix is a mythical firebird that appears from the hot ashes of its burning mother, while its real-life counterpart, the Tongan megapode bird, incubates its eggs in the warm ash of a volcano.

Something fishy
Mermaids are mythical creatures that are said to look like a woman with a fish tail instead of legs. Sailors telling stories of beautiful fish-maidens may have mistaken dugongs or manatees for mermaids.

Long crest formed by first few dorsal fin rays

The oarfish grows up to 56 ft (17 m) in length.

Serpent or not?
The oarfish is the nearest thing to a sea serpent in nature and is longer than any other fish. It normally lives in the depths of the seas, but sometimes comes to the surface.

Camera inside watertight box

Searching for Nessie
This underwater "Creature Camera" was used in the 1970s to look for the mythical Loch Ness Monster. "Nessie" is said to be an immense reptile that lurks in Loch Ness, Britain's largest lake. The camera found nothing.

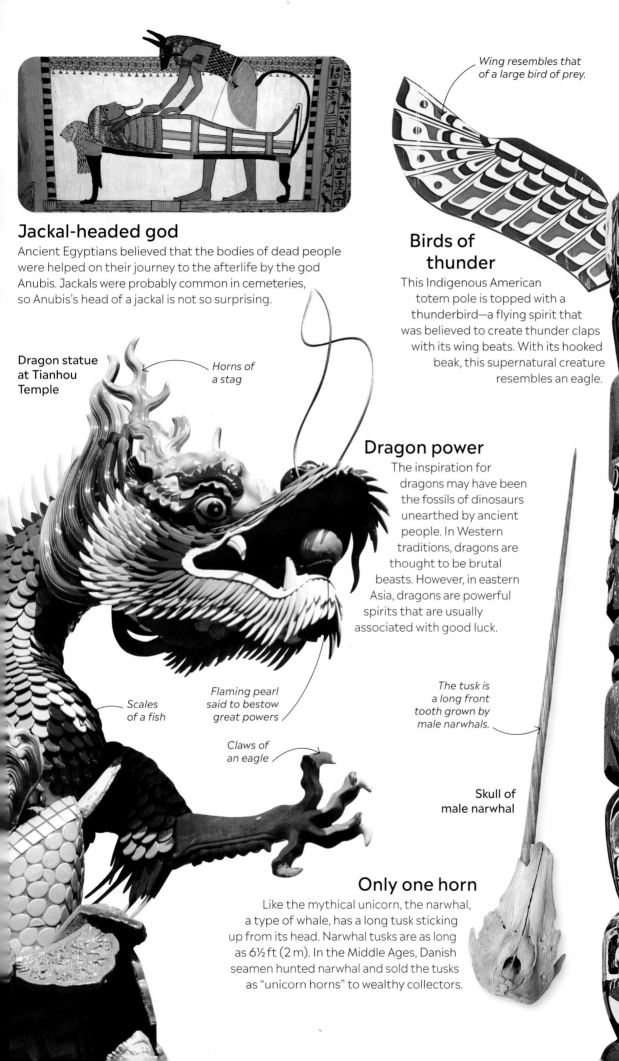

Jackal-headed god

Ancient Egyptians believed that the bodies of dead people were helped on their journey to the afterlife by the god Anubis. Jackals were probably common in cemeteries, so Anubis's head of a jackal is not so surprising.

Dragon statue at Tianhou Temple

Horns of a stag

Birds of thunder

This Indigenous American totem pole is topped with a thunderbird—a flying spirit that was believed to create thunder claps with its wing beats. With its hooked beak, this supernatural creature resembles an eagle.

Wing resembles that of a large bird of prey.

Dragon power

The inspiration for dragons may have been the fossils of dinosaurs unearthed by ancient people. In Western traditions, dragons are thought to be brutal beasts. However, in eastern Asia, dragons are powerful spirits that are usually associated with good luck.

Scales of a fish

Flaming pearl said to bestow great powers

Claws of an eagle

The tusk is a long front tooth grown by male narwhals.

Skull of male narwhal

Only one horn

Like the mythical unicorn, the narwhal, a type of whale, has a long tusk sticking up from its head. Narwhal tusks are as long as 6½ ft (2 m). In the Middle Ages, Danish seamen hunted narwhal and sold the tusks as "unicorn horns" to wealthy collectors.

Record breakers

Among the millions of species that make up the animal kingdom, there are many extraordinary creatures. For example, the cheetah can outrun every other animal on land. Biologists discover new record breakers all the time.

LARGEST COLONY

Argentinian ants
These tiny South American ants have spread to other parts of the world. A supercolony in Europe stretches for 3,730 miles (6,000 km).

Record: Supercolony (billions of ants)
Group: Insects
Habitat: Coast of southern Europe

FASTEST ANIMAL IN WATER

Sailfish
This predatory fish powers through the water with a rapid sweep of its tail and its sword-shaped bill. The sailfish raises its sail-like fin to frighten its prey.

Record: Can reach a speed of 68 mph (110 kph)
Group: Ray-finned fishes
Habitat: Open oceans

LARGEST LAND INVERTEBRATE

Coconut crab
Also known as the robber crab, this crustacean climbs on palm trees to eat fruits. Its large pincers are strong enough to crack coconuts.

Record: Leg span of 35 in (90 cm)
Group: Crustaceans
Habitat: Tropical islands

HOTTEST HABITAT

Pompeii worm
This sea worm lives in the Pacific Ocean, in the hot water emerging from seafloor volcanic vents. The worm converts chemicals in the water into nutrients.

Record: Can survive at 176°F (80°C)
Group: Segmented worms
Habitat: Hydrothermal vents

SMALLEST VERTEBRATE

Brazilian flea toad
This frog is the smallest amphibian. Its tiny feet have just two toes instead of the usual five, and the male is even smaller than the female.

Record: Length of ¼ in (7 mm)
Group: Amphibians
Habitat: Mountain forests of Brazil

LOUDEST ANIMAL

Sperm whale
Sperm whales produce sounds that are louder than a jet engine. Their calls can travel thousands of miles through water.

Record: Can produce sounds of 230 decibels
Group: Cetaceans
Habitat: Open ocean

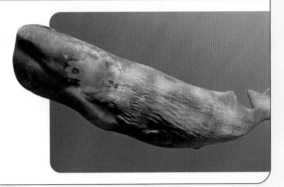

SLOWEST FISH

Seahorse
The seahorse can barely swim. A male seahorse spends its entire adult life in the same cubic yard of water.

Record: 0.0006 mph (0.001 kph)
Group: Ray-finned fishes
Habitat: Seaweed

FASTEST ANIMAL IN AIR

Peregrine falcon
The peregrine falcon preys on other birds in mid-air, plummeting toward them at high speed from far above. By the time the prey sees the falcon, it is too late.

Record: Max speed of 200 mph (325 kph)
Group: Birds
Habitat: Cliffs

LONGEST PREGNANCY

African elephant
The African elephant's pregnancy is the longest. Its calves weigh 220 lb (100 kg) and must be able to stand and walk soon after birth.

Record: Pregnancy lasts 660 days
Group: Mammals
Habitat: African savanna

STRONGEST ANIMAL

Dung beetle
Dung beetles are able to shift dung balls weighing more than 1,000 times their own weight—the equivalent of a human moving six buses at a time.

Record: Pushes 1,141 times its body weight
Group: Insects
Habitat: Grasslands and forests

LARGEST STRUCTURE BY A LIVING THING

Australian Great Barrier Reef
Over a period of about 7,000 years, countless generations of coral polyps have built Australia's Great Barrier Reef into a chain of hundreds of reefs and islands.

Record: Length of 1,615 miles (2,600 km)
Group: Cnidarians
Habitat: Warm, shallow waters

Tree of life

Biologists are still figuring out the relationships between different species and those between larger groups of animals. But they know enough to organize animals into a broad tree of life. Closely related animals are clustered together. Subgroups branch off. This tree begins with sponges, the simplest and, perhaps, oldest animal.

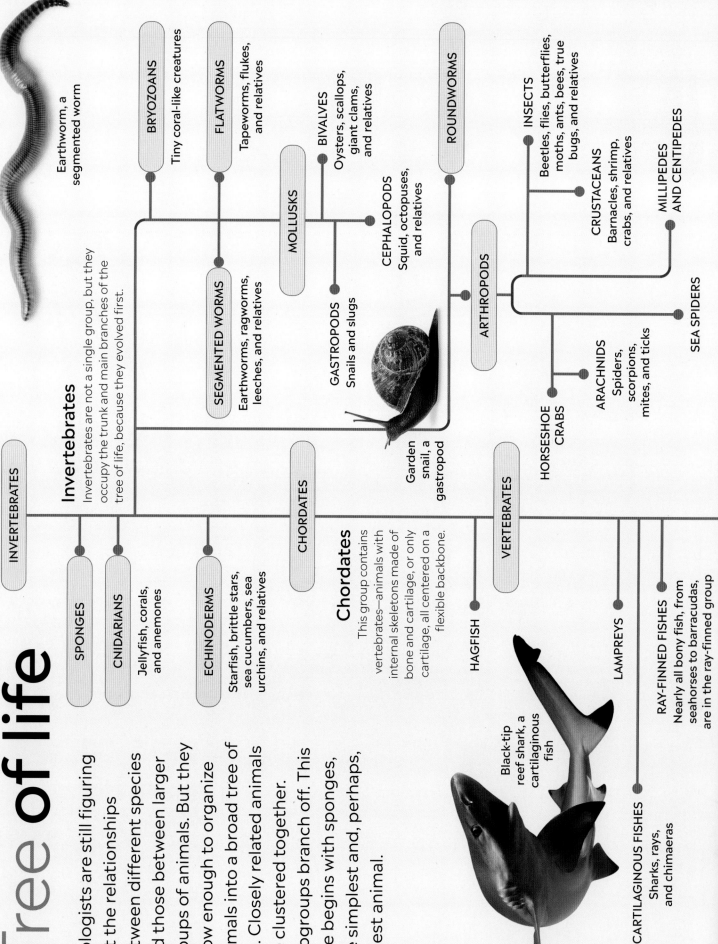

Earthworm, a segmented worm

INVERTEBRATES

Invertebrates

Invertebrates are not a single group, but they occupy the trunk and main branches of the tree of life, because they evolved first.

BRYOZOANS
Tiny coral-like creatures

FLATWORMS
Tapeworms, flukes, and relatives

BIVALVES
Oysters, scallops, giant clams, and relatives

MOLLUSKS

SEGMENTED WORMS
Earthworms, ragworms, leeches, and relatives

CEPHALOPODS
Squid, octopuses, and relatives

GASTROPODS
Snails and slugs

ROUNDWORMS

INSECTS
Beetles, flies, butterflies, moths, ants, bees, true bugs, and relatives

CRUSTACEANS
Barnacles, shrimp, crabs, and relatives

MILLIPEDES AND CENTIPEDES

ARTHROPODS

ARACHNIDS
Spiders, scorpions, mites, and ticks

SEA SPIDERS

HORSESHOE CRABS

Garden snail, a gastropod

SPONGES

CNIDARIANS
Jellyfish, corals, and anemones

ECHINODERMS
Starfish, brittle stars, sea cucumbers, sea urchins, and relatives

CHORDATES

Chordates

This group contains vertebrates—animals with internal skeletons made of bone and cartilage, or only cartilage, all centered on a flexible backbone.

VERTEBRATES

HAGFISH

LAMPREYS

RAY-FINNED FISHES
Nearly all bony fish, from seahorses to barracudas, are in the ray-finned group

CARTILAGINOUS FISHES
Sharks, rays, and chimaeras

Black-tip reef shark, a cartilaginous fish

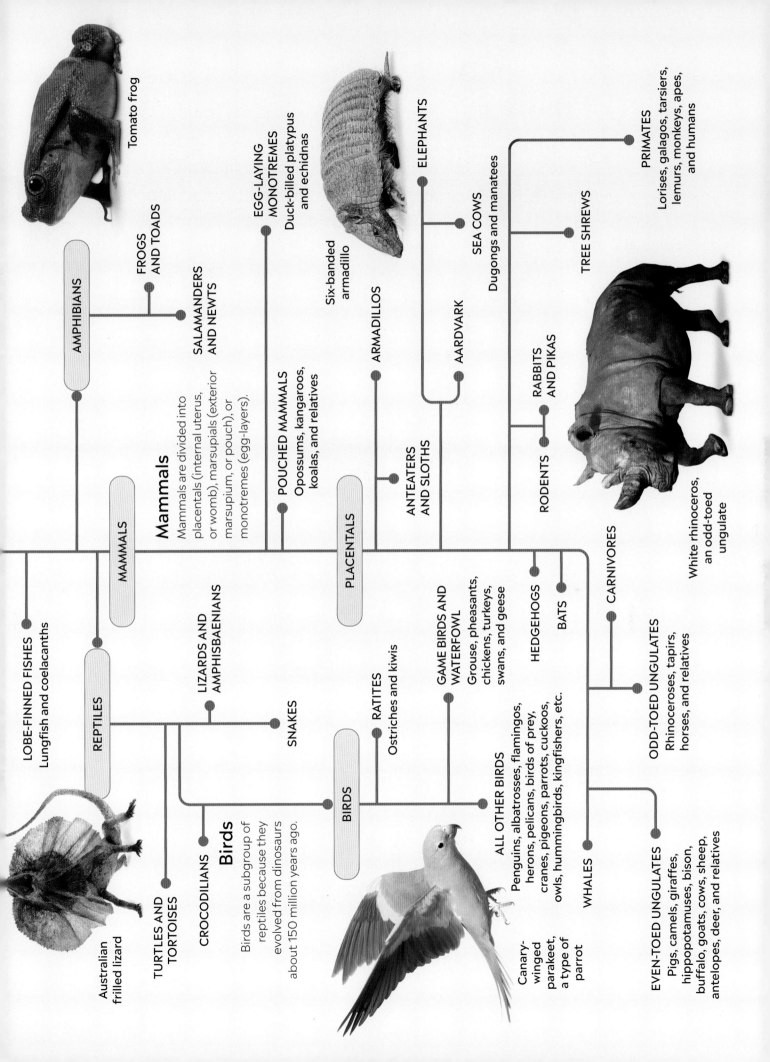

Tomato frog

AMPHIBIANS

FROGS AND TOADS

SALAMANDERS AND NEWTS

EGG-LAYING MONOTREMES
Duck-billed platypus and echidnas

Six-banded armadillo

ELEPHANTS

SEA COWS
Dugongs and manatees

AARDVARK

ARMADILLOS

TREE SHREWS

PRIMATES
Lorises, galagos, tarsiers, lemurs, monkeys, apes, and humans

MAMMALS

Mammals

Mammals are divided into placentals (internal uterus, or womb), marsupials (exterior marsupium, or pouch), or monotremes (egg-layers).

POUCHED MAMMALS
Opossums, kangaroos, koalas, and relatives

PLACENTALS

ANTEATERS AND SLOTHS

RABBITS AND PIKAS

RODENTS

LOBE-FINNED FISHES
Lungfish and coelacanths

REPTILES

LIZARDS AND AMPHISBAENIANS

SNAKES

CROCODILIANS

TURTLES AND TORTOISES

Australian frilled lizard

Birds

Birds are a subgroup of reptiles because they evolved from dinosaurs about 150 million years ago.

BIRDS

RATITES
Ostriches and kiwis

GAME BIRDS AND WATERFOWL
Grouse, pheasants, chickens, turkeys, swans, and geese

HEDGEHOGS

BATS

CARNIVORES

ALL OTHER BIRDS
Penguins, albatrosses, flamingos, herons, pelicans, birds of prey, cranes, pigeons, parrots, cuckoos, owls, hummingbirds, kingfishers, etc.

Canary-winged parakeet, a type of parrot

WHALES

ODD-TOED UNGULATES
Rhinoceroses, tapirs, horses, and relatives

White rhinoceros, an odd-toed ungulate

EVEN-TOED UNGULATES
Pigs, camels, giraffes, hippopotamuses, bison, buffalo, goats, cows, sheep, antelopes, deer, and relatives

Animal watch

Blue tits are attracted to a nut-filled feeder.

Observing animals requires skill and patience. Getting a good look at an animal in its natural habitat can be difficult. Wild animals are wary of anything unusual, but knowing when and where an animal will appear helps us study them in the wild.

Magnifying glass helps study small invertebrates.

Setting the scene

All animals need to eat and they often return to known feeding sites. This works to a watcher's advantage. For example, grizzly bears in Alaska gather near rivers in the fall to catch salmon migrating upstream. People also attract animals, such as blue tits, to a viewing spot by providing food.

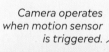

Sun hat provides shade and also breaks up the tell-tale shape of the head.

Small backpack to carry essentials

Walking boots

Camera operates when motion sensor is triggered.

A compact, weight-saving model

Recording wildlife

Camera traps are set in places where animals visit regularly. It automatically films or takes photographs when it detects a nearby animal. A camera trap can be left in place for days or even weeks.

Binoculars allow watchers to see details at a distance

Large grips reduce chances of slipping in mud and on loose stones.

FOLLOWING THE SEASONS

As a region's weather changes with the seasons, so does the behavior of animals living there. A good wildlife watcher will know where a species is likely to be at each time of year. For example, they do not look for European hedgehogs in winter but only in summer, when the ball-shaped nests of these animals can be seen in bushes and thickets.

These common cranes have arrived in northern Europe in early summer to breed. They perform distinctive courtship displays to attract mates.

This flock of pink-footed geese is leaving Greenland in the fall for Europe, where many birdwatchers travel to watch them arrive.

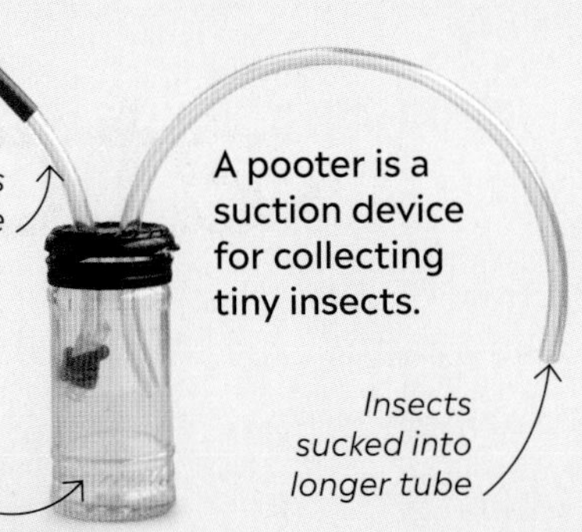

User sucks shorter tube

A pooter is a suction device for collecting tiny insects.

Flask traps insects

Insects sucked into longer tube

Large rucksack to hold gear, water, and food on long trips

Camera to record interesting animals

Long, powerful lens

GPS device pinpoints its exact location, using satellite signals.

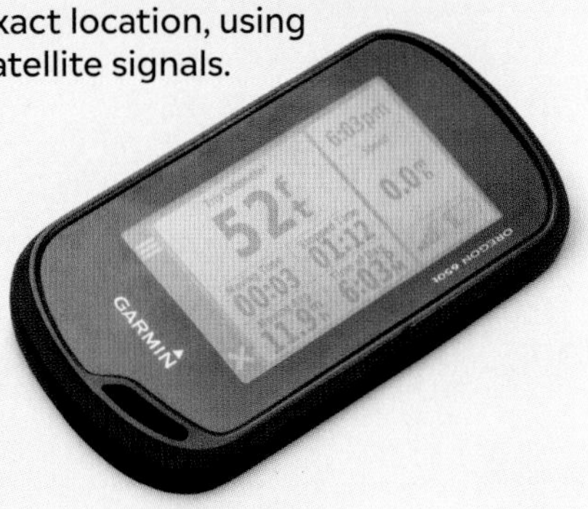

Getting ready

Wildlife watchers carry equipment for finding, viewing, and recording animals in their natural habitats. Nature lovers spend a lot of time outdoors in all kinds of weather. They need warm and dry clothing, that does not make rustling sounds, in muted colors to avoid standing out.

Hide has a camouflage pattern to help it blend in with surroundings.

READING THE SIGNS

Wildlife experts can find animals from the signs they leave behind. Large animals leave distinctive prints in snow and mud, as well as broken twigs and flattened plants. Trackers look for the signs that animals leave for each other, such as dung piles, smelly scents, and scratches in trees.

These marks are left by a red deer, known as an elk in North America, chewing on bark during winter. Fresh marks show that the deer may be nearby.

A black bear marks its territory by gouging deep scratches in soft tree bark with its claws and teeth. The height of the mark shows how tall the bear is.

This tree has been gnawed by a beaver as it collects logs for constructing its dam. This rodent will have dug a channel nearby leading to its pool.

These holes were made by a woodpecker looking for insects under the bark. The noise made by this chiseling gives away the bird's position.

Glossary

Brown fungus growing on log

Algae Organisms that photosynthesize like a plant, but are mostly single-celled. Algae often live in water or damp places.

Aquatic To do with water. Aquatic animals spend most of their time in water.

Artery A blood vessel that carries oxygen-rich blood from the heart to other body organs.

Bacteria Tiny, single-celled organisms that are not plant, animal, or fungus. Bacterial cells are at least 100 times smaller than an animal cell. Most bacteria are harmless, but some cause disease.

Brackish Water that is partly salty and partly fresh. Brackish water is found in coastal swamps and river mouths where fresh water mixes with sea water.

Bioluminescence Ability of some animals to produce light using chemicals or specialized bacteria in their bodies.

Carbon dioxide A gas produced as a waste product by animals when they extract energy by processing sugars and other foods in their bodies. Animals take in oxygen and give out carbon dioxide when they breathe.

Carnivore An animal that mostly eats meat—the flesh of other animals. Carnivores are generally predators, often killing animals that they eat.

Chitin A tough material in the outer body coverings of many invertebrates.

Chromosome A microscopic structure in the cells of all animals that is used as a frame around which long strands of DNA are coiled.

Cold-blooded Also known as ectothermic, a cold-blooded animal is one that cannot maintain a constant body temperature. Instead, its body temperature varies with the environmental conditions.

Corpse The body of a dead animal.

Cretaceous Period The geological period from 145–66 MYA (million years ago). It was the longest period in the Mesozoic Era.

DNA Short for deoxyribonucleic acid, DNA is a complex chemical formed from a chain of four chemical units, or bases. The genetic code of an animal is stored in the way these four bases are ordered in its DNA chains.

Dorsal fin The fin on the back of an aquatic animal, such as a shark or a dolphin. The fin stops the animal from rolling as it swims.

Ectotherm A cold-blooded animal. *Ecto* means "outside" and *therm* is "heat"—an ectotherm uses outside heat.

Chameleon, an ectotherm

Endotherm A warm-blooded animal. *Endo* means "inside"; an endotherm uses its body heat to stay warm.

Enzyme A protein chemical with a specific job to do in an animal's body. Digestive enzymes break up certain foods into simpler ingredients, while other enzymes copy DNA. An enzyme's special shape helps it perform its task.

Evolution A process by which organisms change over a period of time, and across many generations, as they adapt to changes in the environment. New species are often formed in this process.

Extinct A species that has died out.

Fungus An organism that is neither an animal nor a plant. A fungus, such as a mushroom, grows into its food and digests it externally.

Gene A strand of DNA that carries the instructions for a characteristic of an organism—such as the color of a bird's feathers, or the shape of its wings.

Gill The organ used by many aquatic animals to absorb oxygen from water and give out carbon dioxide.

Gizzard A muscular part of a bird's gut used to grind food.

Habitat The place where an animal lives.

Herbivore An animal that only eats plant food. It may eat leaves (folivore), fruits (frugivore), seeds (granivore), sap and juices (exudivore), or roots (radicivore).

Clown fish, a hermaphrodite— changes from male to female

Hermaphrodite An animal that has both male and female sex organs. Some hermaphrodites start life as one sex and change into the other as they grow. Other hermaphrodites have both sets of sex organs at the same time.

Hybrid A cross between two species or breeds. A mule is a hybrid of a horse and a donkey, while a mongrel is a hybrid between dog breeds.

Insulator A substance that stops heat escaping from an animal's body, keeping it warm. Blubber, feathers, and hair are the common insulators found in animals.

Invertebrate Any animal that is not a member of the phylum Chordata. Most of the world's animals are invertebrates.

Keratin A flexible protein present in the external body features of vertebrates, such as hair, feathers, claws, scales, horn sheaths, and fingernails.

Kleptoparasite An animal that survives by stealing food from another hunter, generally of a different species.

Larva The young form of an insect or other invertebrate that looks different to the adult form and also lives in a different way. A caterpillar is an example of a larva.

Toucan's bill contains keratin

Lift force The force that pushes a flying animal off the ground.

Membrane A thin layer or barrier that may allow some substances to pass through.

Microscopic When something is too small to see with the naked eye. A microscope is used to observe it.

Nocturnal Animals that are active at night and sleep during the day.

Nutrients The useful parts of food, such as sugars, proteins, fats, oils, vitamins, and minerals. An animal's digestive system extracts these from food.

Nymph An early stage of development of an insect or other invertebrate that generally looks and lives in the same way as the organism's adult form.

Oxygen A substance used by an animal's body in chemical reactions that release energy from sugars and other foods. It is taken in by breathing in air or absorbing it from water.

Parasite An animal that lives on or in another animal of a different species.

Phylum The largest grouping used to organize, or classify, life. There are dozens of animal phyla. Some of the main ones are Arthropoda (insects and crabs), Mollusca (snails and squid), and Chordata (vertebrates).

Pigments Chemicals that give color to an organism. It may be the main function of the pigment or the coloration may be incidental. For example, the pigments in the eye are used as light detectors.

Predator An animal that hunts other animals for food.

Protein A complex chemical found in all life forms, but mostly in animals. Proteins help build body parts. Enzymes are examples of proteins.

Saliva The liquid produced by salivary glands in the mouth of an animal to moisten food, making it easier to swallow and digest.

Scute An armored plate of bone covered in skin or horny keratin. A turtle shell is made up of interlocking scutes, while a crocodile's body is protected by ridges of scutes.

Species A group of animals that look the same and live in the same way, and also breed with each other to produce offspring that will be able to reproduce themselves.

Symbiosis A partnership between two animals of different species that live with each other. In most cases, each animal provides a service or benefit to the other in the relationship.

Territory An area of land or water defended by an animal. Territory is used as a feeding space or as an area for mates to live, and unwanted members of the same species are driven away.

Tetrapod A vertebrate with four limbs.

Urine The liquid waste of mammals and other animals. While dung, or feces, is the undigested materials in food, urine is the waste removed from the blood and body tissues.

Vein A blood vessel that carries oxygen-poor blood from the body organs toward the heart.

Venom Poison that is produced by an animal and injected into another by a bite, scratch, or sting. Venom is used in hunting as well as in defense.

Vertebrate An animal with a backbone—a set of small vertebrae that connect to form a flexible spine. The vertebrate groups are fish, amphibians, reptiles, birds, and mammals.

Warm-blooded Also known as endothermic, a warm-blooded animal is one that controls its body temperature internally, using a lot of energy to heat or cool its body, so it stays at more or less the same temperature whatever the weather conditions at that time.

Turtle shell contains scutes

Leopard, a predator, with its kill

Index

Acknowledgments

The publisher would like to thank the following for their help with making the book: Sheila Collins, Tanvi Sahu, Shahid Qureshi, and Diya Varma for design and editorial assistance; Vishal Bhatia for DTP assistance and Vikram Singh for Hi-Res work; John Friend for proofreading; and Helen Peters for the index.

The publisher would like to thank the following for their kind permission to reproduce their photographs:

(Key: a-above; b-below/bottom; c-center; f-far; l-left; r-right; t-top)

Alamy Images: Amazon-Images 23tr, CML Images 59br, Avalon / Bruce Coleman Inc 24bc, Mark Conlin / VWPICS / Visual&Written SL 42bc, Custom Life Science Images 11br, Stephen Dalton / Photoshot Holdings Ltd 39tr, Imagebroker 33cra, Chris Mattison 32tr, Mauritius images GmbH 32b, MicroScan / Phototake Inc. 12br, Karen Miller Photography 68cl, Minden Pictures 39cl, 61cla, 64bc, Todd Mintz 42crb, Mira 26tl, Richard Mittleman / Gon2Foto 11tr, V. Muthuraman / SuperStock 36bl, NaturePics 64cra, Matthew Oldfield 24cr, Michael Patrick O'Neill 10–11c, Clément Philippe / Arterra Picture Library 69crb, The Sarigua Collection by Oyvind Martinsen 69b, Soeren Stache / dpa 42cl, Bjorn Svensson / Science Photo Library 69br, Duncan Usher 48–49bc, WaterFrame 65tc, Dave Watts 13cr, 17cl; **Alan McFadyen, www.scottishphotograhyhides.co.uk:** 45br; **Ardea:** Steve Downer 26bl, Ferrero-Labat 22–23c, François Gohier 48bl; **Corbis:** Hinrich Baesemann / DPA 30–31b, Hal Beral 9tr, Nigel Cattlin / Visuals Unlimited 15clb, Ralph Clevenger 42–43, Dr John D. Cunningham / Visuals Unlimited 69cr, Mark Downey 2bc, 24tl, Macduff Everton 53cla, Michael & Patricia Fogden 18–19, 36cra, Tim Graham 68br, James Hager / Robert Harding World Imagery 23c, Dave Hamman / Gallo Images 55crb, Martin Harvey 37br, Martin Harvey / Gallo Images 22bl, Eric & David Hosking 4tl, 48cl, Jason Isley - Scubazoo / Science Faction 42tl, Wolfgang Kaehler 29cl, Karen Kasmauski / Science Faction 61tr, Thomas Kitchin & Victoria Hurst / First Light 13br, Peter Kneffel / DPA 54tl, Stephen J. Krasemann / All Canada Photos 34cl, Frans Lanting 4bl, 31cl, 33br, 60br, Frans Lemmens 49cra, Wayne Lynch / All Canada Photos 31cr, Dan McCoy - Rainbow / Science Faction 50cla, Joe McDonald 10br, 38cl, Tim Mckulka / UNMIS / Reuters 52–53, Dong Naide / Xinhua Press 53tr, David A. Northcott 6tl, Michael Redmer / Visuals Unlimited 6bc (*plethodon jordani*), 9tl, Bryan Reynolds / Science Faction 59fcra, David Scharf / Science Faction 55cl, Shoot 60tr, Jeff Vanuga 58t, Carlos Villoch / Specialist Stock 26–27, Visuals Unlimited 7cr, 44tl, Stuart Westmorland 8clb, 10bl, Ralph White 62bl, Lawson Wood 27c, Norbert Wu / Science Faction 20bl, 47c; **Depositphotos Inc:**

Charmboyz 60bc; **Dreamstime.com:** Tony Campbell 15br, Chernetskaya 68cr, Dalia Kvedaraite 30cl, Slowmotiongli 55cla, Urospoteko 39br, Valentyn640 20cr; **Rylee Brooke Kamahele:** Sasha Kamahele 61br; **Dorling Kindersley:** ESPL - modelmaker 50r, Exmoor Zoo, Devon 15cra (Azara's Agouti), Hunterian Museum (University of Glasgow) 4br, 17ca, Trustees of the National Museums Of Scotland 17crb, Natural History Museum, London 8cra, 12fbr, 13tl, 16cra, 44c, 58br (two larger coackroaches), 58fcrb (larger cockroach), 59c (larger cockroach), 68ftr, based on a photo by David Robinson / The Open University 33crb, Rough Guides 50bl, Stanley Park, Totem Park, Vancouver, British Columbia 2l, 63r, University College, London 51l, Whipsnade Zoo, Bedfordshire Barrie Watts 66ca, 67cra, Jerry Young 4tr, 4cra, 10–11tc, 24ca, 37ca, 56cla, 67tl; **FLPA:** Ingo Arndt / Minden Pictures 37tr, Flip De Nooyer/ Minden 50r, Michael Durham / Minden Pictures 19cra (leeches), Suzi Eszterhas / Minden Pictures 47br, John Holmes 30–31tc, Donald M. Jones / Minden Pictures 69cra, Mark Moffett / Minden Pictures 29tr, Jurgen & Christine Sohns 35cra, Konrad Wothe/ Minden Pictures 45cra, 65cla, Norbert Wu/ Minden Pictures 47clb; **Getty Images:** Abubekir Albayati/500px 31tc, Gerry Bishop/ Visuals Unlimited 46br, The Bridgeman Art Library 57cr, Stephen Dalton / Minden Pictures 29br, George Day / Gallo Images 8tl, David Doubilet / National Geographic 8–9bc, Georgette Douwma / Photographer's Choice 27bc, Richard du Toit / Gallo Images 47tr, Guy Edwardes / The Image Bank 59tl, Eurasia / Robert Harding World Imagery 62–63bc, George Grall / National Geographic 18clb,

Louis-Laurent Grandadam / The Image Bank 55b, Henry Guttmann / Hulton Archive 15tc, Hulton Archive 59bl, David Maitland 44crb, Joe McDonald / Visuals Unlimited 46–47, Alan McFadyen 45l, Bruno Morandi / The Image Bank 28tl, Marwan Naamani / AFP 33tr, Iztok Noc / Photodisc 56–57, Radius Images 65br, 71cra, David Silverman 29tl, Keren Su 7tr, U.S. Navy 54bl, Mario Vazquez / AFP 43tr, Gary Vestal / Photographer's Choice 7l, 25b, Alex Wild / Visuals Unlimited, Inc. 65cb; **Getty Images / iStock:** Dennis Stogsdill 34–35c; **imagequestmarine.com:** 64br; **Keertana Jillella and Sravani Jillella:** Prashant Ramars Jillella 11bl; **Darren Naish:** 17tr; **NASA:** GSFC/ Craig Mayhew & Robert Simmon 51t; **naturepl.com:** Chris Gomersall 41tc, Andy Rouse 36–37c, Kim Taylor 25tr, 38b (dragonflies), Dave Watts 40tc, 40tr; **Photolibrary:** Kathie Atkinson/ Oxford Scientific (OSF) 40clb, Stefan Auth/ Imagebroker.net 54br, Paulo de Oliveira/ Oxford Scientific (OSF) 62cla, David B. Fleetham / Oxford Scientific (OSF) 27cr, François Gilson / Bios 40bl, jspix jspix/ Imagebroker.net 12tr, Steven Kazlowski/ Alaskastock 60–61c, Morales Morales / Age fotostock 64clb, Rolf Nussbaumer/ Imagebroker.net 21clb, Jean-Paul Chatagnon / Bios 49tr, Gerhard Schultz/ Oxford Scientific (OSF) 40crb, Gerhard Schulz / Bios 41crb, M. Varesvuo 20–21tc; **Justin Sather:** Daniel Chàvez Jàcome 36bc; **Science Photo Library:** Susumu Nishinaga 12bc, Power & Syred 29tl, 46tr, Volker Steger 21crb, 21fcrb; **Shutterstock.com:** epic_images 51br, marekuliasz 69c; **SuperStock:** Minden Pictures 33clb.

All other images © Dorling Kindersley

WHAT WILL YOU EYEWITNESS NEXT?

 THE AMAZON
 AMERICAN REVOLUTION
 ANCIENT EGYPT
 ANCIENT GREECE
 ANCIENT ROME
 ANIMAL
 ARCTIC & ANTARCTIC

 BIRD
 CAT
 THE CIVIL WAR
 CLIMATE CHANGE
 CRYSTAL & GEM
 DINOSAUR
 THE ELEMENTS

 FISH
 FLIGHT
 FOSSIL
 HORSE
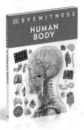 HUMAN BODY
 HURRICANE & TORNADO
 INSECT

 KNIGHT
 NATIONAL PARKS
 NATURAL DISASTERS
 OCEAN
 PLANETS
 REPTILE
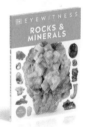 ROCKS & MINERALS

 SHARK
 SOCCER
 TITANIC
 TRAIN
 UNIVERSE
 VIKING
 VOLCANO & EARTHQUAKE

 WEATHER
 WONDERS OF THE WORLD
 WORLD WAR I
 WORLD WAR II

Also available:

Eyewitness Amphibian
Eyewitness Ancient China
Eyewitness Ancient Civilizations
Eyewitness Arms and Armor
Eyewitness Astronomy
Eyewitness Aztec, Inca & Maya
Eyewitness Baseball
Eyewitness Bible Lands
Eyewitness Car

Eyewitness Castle
Eyewitness Chemistry
Eyewitness Dance
Eyewitness Earth
Eyewitness Eagle and Birds of Prey
Eyewitness Electricity
Eyewitness Endangered Animals
Eyewitness Forensic Science
Eyewitness Gandhi
Eyewitness Great Scientists

Eyewitness Islam
Eyewitness Judaism
Eyewitness Jungle
Eyewitness Medieval Life
Eyewitness Mesopotamia
Eyewitness Money
Eyewitness Mummy
Eyewitness Mythology
Eyewitness North American Indian
Eyewitness Pirate

Eyewitness Plant
Eyewitness Prehistoric Life
Eyewitness Presidents
Eyewitness Robot
Eyewitness Science
Eyewitness Shakespeare
Eyewitness Skeleton
Eyewitness Soldier
Eyewitness Space Exploration
Eyewitness Vietnam War